FOR ALL TIME

A Complete Guide to Writing
Your Family History

✶ Charley Kempthorne ✶

Boynton/Cook Publishers
HEINEMANN
Portsmouth, NH

Boynton/Cook Publishers
A subsidiary of Reed Elsevier Inc.
361 Hanover Street
Portsmouth, NH 03801-3912

Offices and agents throughout the world

© 1996 by Charley Kempthorne

All rights reserved. No part of this book may be reproduced in any form or by any electronic or mechanical means, including information storage and retrieval systems, without permission in writing from the publisher, except by a reviewer, who may quote brief passages in a review.

The author and publisher wish to thank those who have generously given permission to reprint borrowed material:

Fig. 2–1, *Canvassing for a Vote* by George Caleb Bingham, 1852, courtesy of The Nelson-Atkins Museum of Art, Kansas City, Missouri (Purchase: Nelson Trust) 54-9

Library of Congress Cataloging-in-Publication Data

Kempthorne, Charley.
    For all time : a complete guide to writing your family history /
Charley Kempthorne.
        p.   cm.
    Includes bibliographical references.
    ISBN 0-86709-381-1
        1. Genealogy—Authorship.   2. United States—Genealogy—Handbooks,
manuals, etc.   I. Title.
CS6.K46   1996
929'.1—dc20   96-7822
                                                                              CIP

EDITOR: *Peter R. Stillman*
PRODUCTION: *Vicki Kasabian*
BOOK AND COVER DESIGN: *Jenny Jensen Greenleaf*
MANUFACTURING: *Louise Richardson*

Printed in the United States of America on acid-free paper

99 98 97   DA   4 5

To my wife
June Fritz Kempthorne
in love and loyalty

CONTENTS

ACKNOWLEDGMENTS

While writing family history can make you realize how much you owe to others, so does writing a book *about* family history. In 1991 my wife June and I started a monthly publication we called *LifeStory Magazine* to help people who wanted to write personal and family history. I am grateful to *LifeStory* subscribers who took me seriously when I said the magazine was interactive. I invited them to send me some or all of their writings for my criticism and comment. The idea was that the magazine would become a kind of classroom, that we would publish in its pages excerpts from their work so that everyone else could read and learn from them.

Subscribers wrote to me from all over—from Modesto, California, Pocahontas, Iowa, from Harlingen, Texas, and Enfield, New Hampshire. I received letters from Florida, Wisconsin, Canada, and even a retired attorney who wrote me in a beautiful but wavering hand from India that he regrettably would not be able to write any family history because he felt he was too old. Subscribers sent me pages from their family histories to read and comment on, and offered also their own comments and encouragement about the magazine. I have been and continue to be delighted and moved by the histories they write. Most of what I know about family history I have learned from them. Many have done me the honor of becoming friends through the mail.

I am greatly indebted to three old friends and former colleagues from my classroom teaching days. The first is Elizabeth Verschelden, now of the University of Kansas, the kind of encouraging and creatively sustaining administrator every teacher dreams of. In 1977 we started the Harvest Program at the Adult Learning Center here in Manhattan, possibly the first reminiscence workshop in the nation.

Although Harvest did not survive the funding cuts to public education of the early 1980s, its goals and ideals certainly did. *LifeStory* and this book are a direct outgrowth of my experience in Harvest and a conscious attempt to further its goals and ideals.

The second old friend I want to thank is Dave Wood, the books editor of the *Star-Tribune of the Twin Cities* of Minneapolis and St. Paul, a friend and colleague from our days teaching together at the University of Wisconsin—Stevens Point. Dave wrote about *LifeStory* and thereby allowed me to reach a much wider audience than I otherwise would have.

Finally, my third friend to thank is Toby Fulwiler, now of the University of Vermont, and another friend and colleague at Stevens Point. Toby was interested in *LifeStory* from its beginning and he encouraged me to write this book.

I also want to thank my closest friends—my family—for allowing me to endlessly invade their privacy to write about them in the pages of *LifeStory* and here: my mother Lillian Kempthorne; my daughter Leslie Kempthorne; my sons Daniel, Benjamin, and Rip Kempthorne; and my wife June Kempthorne.

PREFACE

Suddenly we have a past. We are interested in our personal origins. Genealogy is one of the most popular and fastest-growing hobbies in America. Its practitioners are going at it with the passion of a quest rather than a mere hobby. But just a few short years ago, especially here in the United States, it seemed we had only a future and that we were not interested in our past. We had no use for it. We were a people on the move. Why the change?

In talking with others around the United States, I have heard again and again of Alex Haley's great book *Roots*. In 1977 this book was made into a TV series that enthralled the nation. I remember how we watched night after night, engrossed in the story of one African American's family history, going back to an ancestor's capture and sale as a slave.

But I don't think this story by itself created the interest in writing family history, or what the writer Bob Greene has called "the memoir movement." *Roots* galvanized us, made us aware that all of us, not just those of African American descent, have a past that we are in danger of losing. *Roots* also made us aware that the knowledge of our past could be deeply satisfying; it could fill a need.

This need isn't peculiar to the United States; it's happening all over the world—particularly among the industrialized and so-called advanced societies. We have advanced into a state of rootlessness, and we are in danger of losing our place in the world, just as a few hundred years ago the African family of Alex Haley lost theirs. If we don't know where we come from, the saying goes, we won't know where we're going.

Another proverbial bit of wisdom has it that when a person dies

a whole library dies with him. Great advances in information technology have made the recording of this history easy. But the information, the most significant part of it, is in our heads. How do we
get it out of our heads and down on paper? To show you how to do
that easily and naturally is the work of this book.

Family History
and Its Importance

History Is a Story

Many of us leave school with the idea that history is like the game of Trivial Pursuit: the date Washington was inaugurated, the person who invented the steamboat, the name of the battleship on which the Japanese surrendered to the Allies in World War II. I guess that's what we crammed in our heads the night before examinations. In this way, history is like a pill that is good for us but that may have unfortunate side effects. Yet no historian, history teacher, or serious student of history would say that names and dates and places are what history is all about. History is a story, a narrative of the past. Columbus set off to discover America in 1492 with the *Pinta, Niña* and *Santa Maria*, but facts like these are only bits of information. History makes use of this information in telling the story. The story of how Columbus discovered America is much more complicated and much more interesting.

This distinction between information and story is especially important in family history. If we use the narrow history-as-data definition in our family history, we'll come up with the barest of family trees: who our great-grandparents were, when and where they were married, and when and where they were buried. This information is important stuff, no doubt, but not a story; the facts provide only an outline or a suggestion of a story. Information raises questions: Why did Columbus sail west? How did he feel about what he found? How did the rest of the world at that time react to his discoveries? These are the truly interesting questions that real history answers.

I know that sometimes family historians will look at their schedule and say to themselves, "Well, I don't know how much time I can give to this project, so I'll just put down 'the facts' and then if I have more time later I'll fill things in." And so they research and write down when and where mom and dad were married. I don't want to say accurate facts aren't important, but I do question priorities here. The facts, or at least the important facts, of mom and dad's marriage were not where and when it took place but what they made of it. If you have an hour to spend on their history and you use it to resolve a question about a date or a place, then you have ignored what is important. It is better to spend your time writing something like this:

> Dad was always the first one up. He would rise while it was still dark and dress and go immediately to the barn to do the milking and feed the cows. When he got back to the house Mom was up and had a fire going in the big wood cookstove and the kitchen was warm as toast. Since I was the oldest I was up then too, setting the table and bringing in more wood. Mom would pour Dad a hot cup of coffee and he would sit at the head of the table and they'd talk about the condition of the cows and other animals while she prepared breakfast.

These are the important facts of their life that you should get down first—what their daily life was actually like.

Re-create Your Family's Experience

The data needs to be in your family history also, but that's just the beginning. You need to bring your family history to life by re-creating it. This may seem like a big job and one you hardly bargained for, but in fact it is much easier, more fun, and far more rewarding. I think you'll find the phrase "to re-create experience" a useful and convincing definition of what we ought to do when we sit down to write family history. This can be illustrated by an excerpt from the autobiography of Howard Foster, a retired postal worker from Minnesota. Note that Howard gives information about his family life, but he does it in an indirect, interesting way, and, especially important, he re-creates that life in words. He invites the reader to participate in the experience with him:

> I awoke to the shrill cries of the blue jays in the stately elm trees up and down the street. Church bells were ringing. It

was Sunday morning, the start of another winter day in the small Minnesota town of Owatonna.

My upstairs bedroom was cold. We didn't have heat in the second floor of our house, but I was snug and warm under several quilts and flannel blankets, lying on my back and gazing at the low ceiling. I could hear a squirrel scurrying across the shingles. I bet he's cold, I thought, and on his way back to his warm nest.

Mother called up the stairs. "Time to get up! Breakfast!"

Five minutes passed, then she called again. "Howard Foster, you get out of bed this minute and come to breakfast."

I jumped out of bed, grabbed my clothes, and ran down the hall to the bathroom. It was unheated except when we lit the kerosene heater to bathe in the old clawfoot tub. I dressed quickly and ran downstairs into a warm world filled with tantalizing odors of eggs, bacon, and toast to tempt my big teenage appetite.

My dad and my nine-year-old sister Hattie were already eating. We sat at the dropleaf kitchen table with its many coats of paint and well-scrubbed oilcloth cover. The paint on the legs had dried in long runs—Mother never quite got the knack of a neat paint job. Next to the table was a tall steam radiator, its exposed pipes running from the floor to the high ceiling. On top of the radiator was a pan of water to add moisture to the dry winter air. A linoleum rug with intricately painted patterns that didn't make much sense covered most of the floor.

The kitchen cabinet across the room wasn't built in but stood against the wall like a piece of furniture. Alongside this was the gas range with its oven on one side. Then came Mother's new pride and joy, her first refrigerator. A doorway in one corner led to a small pantry, which held most of the dishes, pots and pans, dried and canned foods, and at times a chocolate cake which I would raid. Dad usually had a big wedge of cheddar cheese. He never liked cheese cold from the fridge; he wanted to eat it when it was near room temperature. He and I would often have an evening snack of a thick piece of cheese and a slice of mild onion between bread. We had driven to several small country cheese factories, sampling until he found just the right well-aged cheddar. He would buy from twenty to fifty pounds in a wedge from a wheel of cheese.

On another wall was the sink, a big shallow thing. In addition to the hot and cold faucets, a hand pump was on the drainboard to draw rainwater from the cistern outside. My sisters always wanted soft water for washing their hair. The only trouble was that the old cistern was usually half full of leaves and mud from the roof gutters and downspouts that drained into it.

Next to the sink was the basement door and the steps that led down there to shelves at one end that held hundreds of quarts of tomatoes, corn, beets, green beans, peas, sauerkraut, peaches, pears, and then the smaller jars of jams, jelly, and relishes. Gunnysacks of potatoes were on the floor, enough to feed a small army.

There is plenty of family history information here: Howard didn't come at first call to breakfast, the family didn't have central heat, the cellar contained much of the produce, and so on. But above all, the author is re-creating a moment in time, presenting an experience for us to feel and think about rather than merely feeding us information or even ideas. Earlier I said that the need to re-create the past is even more important in family history than it is in academic history. Family history puts far more emphasis on re-creation and less on interpretation. You may well read a history of the Civil War to understand better its causes. The historian may even organize the book around certain ideas. But in family history, there is much more emphasis on simply showing the reader what the past has been like.

If history exists to show us the past so that we can learn from it, then it seems reasonable to ask that it show us that past. In the excerpt above, Howard Foster shows us what his life was like in 1941. If he had merely given us data rather than a narrative, we would have no feel for his life. Intellectual, analytic, or merely informational family history is not enough.

History Isn't Just Ancient History

Nor should the writing of family history be limited to what happened generations ago. The story of the recent past is also family history: grandparents, parents, and even the rising generation. Many genealogists now advise starting with one's own life and working backwards in time. The logic of this is inescapable: those who are dead will stay dead. All that they have to offer the historian will remain in place. But those who are alive have a huge amount of family history in their heads that can still be captured. It is the quest for this that sends many historians out to the field with a cassette recorder, camera, video camcorder, and/or paper and pen.

Even so, individuals will have different emphases. Some are still primarily interested in the history of the deceased members of their family. The great majority focus on telling the story of their own early life, often starting with a brief history of their parents' courtship and marriage. More and more come right down into the present to tell about their own children and grandchildren. Younger historians especially seem to be mostly interested in chronicling the immediate past: what one of the children did yesterday or how the visit with grandmother went. All of these diverse approaches are valid so long as they share the wish to capture on paper the stories.

I will be a failure and you will have wasted your time and money unless this book gets you started *writing* family history. Therefore, I'm going to ask you from time to time to stop reading and do a little writing. These are not exercises I'm asking you to write, nor is this a textbook or workbook. I will ask you to write about your own family spontaneously and off the cuff. Please don't revise even if you have the urge to. Just write. Writing without thinking much about it is part of what this book is trying to show you how to do. That's goal number one. Goal number two is to give you a break from the reading, and goal number three is to have a pile of your family's history already written by the time you finish with the book.

Here is what I'd like you to do. Start a page with the heading "Journal" and write down today's date. Use whatever you're accustomed to using to write with: pen, typewriter, or word processor—it doesn't matter. As you read and come to one of the writing suggestions like the one below, do your writing in this journal. Keeping a journal or *journaling*, as some call it, is the royal road to writing family history. I'll have lots more to say about that later on.

☞ SUGGESTION:

Make a list of family stories you'd like to see written up. Don't list things you feel are important and ought to be written up so much as things you'd like to write up, even if they seem mundane and ordinary. You should be able to think of at least half a dozen such stories that have been told and retold in your family that you'd like to make sure don't get lost. They might be full-blown stories, brief anecdotes, or only glimpses of your family's life. Don't ignore ideas merely because you think they're too short.

History and Building a Sense of Family

Not long ago my youngest son Rip, age sixteen, came to the dinner table one evening with a yellowed piece of paper in his hand. Grinning, he handed it to me to read. I have reproduced this "document" (see Fig. 1–1).

Though this paper was written by his big sister shortly after he was born, it was the first time Rip had seen it. He had found it in a large wooden box we call the "archives coffin" where we keep miscellaneous family memorabilia. None of us had seen the paper since it had been written some fourteen years before, and we were quite pleased. We were so pleased in fact that after dinner we phoned Leslie, my daughter (she had adopted the name Kelly as a child, as children will sometimes do), at her home in Seattle and reminded her of it by reading it to her. She was pleased too. We were all moved, we looked at one another with big smiles, and perhaps my wife and I, softies that we are, had a tear in our eyes.

What occurred was of course not unusual. It happens all the time in families. Yet it was a moment that reinforced family solidarity and our love and respect for each other. It was a moment of family bonding. This is the sort of family event that makes one able to go forth into a hostile universe and find meaning and significance in life. We all felt revalidated as human beings as a result of examining this document.

I use the word *document* advisedly. I think that these documents function within the family in the same way that important documents of our common history function within the nation. We put such national historical documents in a temperature- and humidity-controlled glass case in a museum and guard them well. We would consider it a travesty of our history to do otherwise. Yet look how we treat the documents of our family history. Imagine going to the Smithsonian or the Library of Congress and asking to see the correspondence between Washington and Jefferson and being told that it was somewhere in the attic in an old shoebox! Perhaps every home

by Kelly $ ☺!!

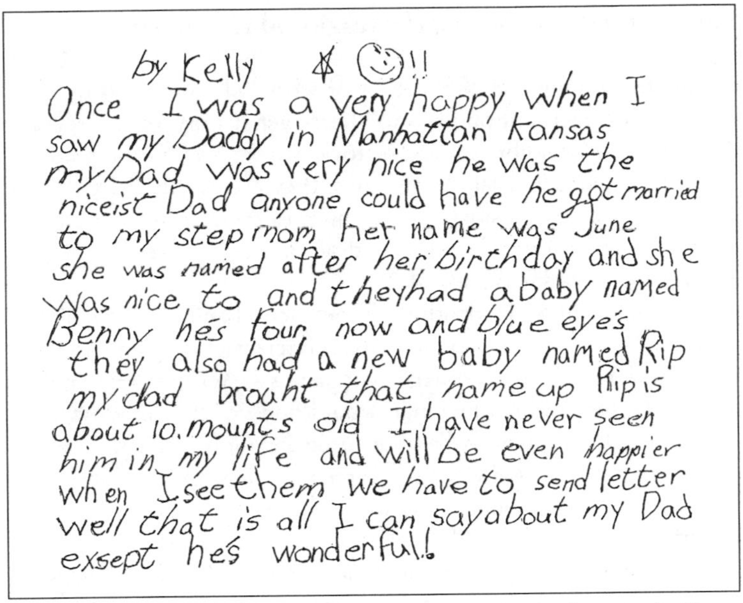

Once I was a very happy when I saw my Daddy in Manhattan kansas my Dad was very nice he was the niceist Dad anyone could have he got married to my step mom her name was June she was named after her birthday and she was nice to and theyhad a baby named Benny hes four now and blue eyes they also had a new baby named Rip my dad broaht that name up Rip is about 10.mounts old I have never seen him in my life and will be even happier when I see them we have to send letter well that is all I can sayabout my Dad exsept hes wonderfull

FIG. 1–1   A child's school paper written about her new baby brother is a valuable "document" of family history.

should have a room or corner set aside that is, in effect, a museum of family history.

We can learn from our family history just as we do from our national history. I hope it won't be taken as unpatriotic of me if I suggest that family history is more important than any other history simply because family is the fundamental, rock-bottom unit of society. We are all familiar with some of the proverbs like "Those who do not understand the past are condemned to repeat it," and "Unless we know where we've been, we won't know where we're going." These sentiments apply to family history too. We may not study our family history, but it will be meaningful just the same. It may well be that the great surge of interest in family history in our time is due to this deep and basic need to see ourselves as part of a process that gives meaning to our discrete, individual lives.

How many criminals come from strong and nurturing families? Very few. Most come from families whose members do not support and nourish each other. It's enough to say that history is an important tool for making a family function better by improving one's sense of family.

Family History and the Professional Historian

Finally, the writing and publication of works of family history may well be a distinct contribution to the larger history of the region. Though most local libraries and historical societies lack the funds to purchase individual or family histories, they are usually delighted to be given a copy. Professional historians must go to primary sources if they are to write original history, and often these sources are the private records of ordinary individuals.

You may think that nothing about your family or your life is noteworthy and would be of no general interest. "How is my life any different from a thousand others?" you may ask. Yet that very similarity may be the reason a historian would find yours of interest. History, after all, is about ordinary people far more than it is about unique and distinct individuals. Moreover, some of the things you have lived through, some of the work you have done, or the places you have been may be valid subjects for professional research.

My life has been as humdrum as any. Yet as a boy I grew up with a job in an old-fashioned (even then) letterpress print shop, and a detailed and even clinical memoir about that experience would probably be of interest to someone writing a history of letterpress printing in that era. I could write about my memories of my father's medical practice, when I often accompanied him on house calls. I could write about rural schools in my boyhood Indiana from the point of view of a pupil, or World War II through the eyes of a child on the homefront. In your life there are similar windows, and your careful observations might be of considerable value to the professional historian.

☛ SUGGESTION:

Make your own list of half a dozen areas you might be considered an expert in. Be specific and don't worry about whether the area has historical significance (or any significance). Everything that humans do is grist for history's mill. You don't have to be the world's foremost authority, just someone who knows the subject well enough to write about it in detail. Fishing pasture streams in Wisconsin, being a member of the military department of a troop transport in the 1950s, making a dress from a pattern, and knowing how to do a popular high school and college dance of the 1940s would, in the proper context, all have historical significance.

Writing Family History and Personal Values

When I started a reminiscence writing workshop back in the 1970s I had the experience again and again of talking to elderly people, many of them in their eighties and nineties, and even a few centenarians. Not infrequently these people were in state of mild to moderate depression and weren't at first interested in being interviewed about their lives.

When initially asked to tell about their lives, they would make comments like, "Who, me? Why? I haven't done anything." One man insisted that his life "did not have a speck of significance."

"Have you any children?" I asked him.

"Why, of course. They've all grown up and moved away, though."

"And do you have grandchildren?"

That was when he reached for his wallet. He had eleven grandchildren, as a matter of fact. "This is the newest," he said, pulling out one of the photos and handing it to me. "Four months old."

I nodded. "And they don't have a speck of significance?"

He did a double take. First I thought he was going to hit me. Then he laughed a long, hearty laugh. "Well, you got me, didn't you?" he said.

After that he gave me a wonderful interview. He started talking about his three sons and the trouble he and his wife had raising them in the Depression years, how they had nothing to eat but what they could raise and shoot, how World War II came along and they lost their oldest in the Pacific, how they moved away from home then, and he took a job in the city. They eventually bought a home and made a life there. "You've had quite a significant life, then," I said at the end of the interview, shaking his hand. He laughed again and didn't deny it. In just the brief hour we had reviewed his life together, he had been reminded of just how important his life had been.

I have met a few people who did not want to talk about their past. "It was so bad I don't want to think about it," an old man once told me. I had to respect that, of course. After all, he knew what he could handle and what he couldn't. But I learned that even those people who thought their past bad came to feel that it was not so bad as they had believed in telling about it over several sessions or writing about it extensively. Usually, in fact, the telling of a difficult tale is redeeming.

When someone subscribes to my magazine *LifeStory*, along with their first issue I send a survey form that asks them to list their reasons in order of their importance for wanting to write family history. You might wish to consider yours now. The options I list are:

1. to review my own life to understand it better
2. to pass on family stories and/or my own story to my family
3. to leave a historical account
4. for the pleasure of reminiscing
5. for the pleasure of writing
6. to give an honest account of my life

Nine out of ten who respond will list number two as most important, with number one somewhere near the bottom, if it is checked at all. This doesn't surprise me. The majority of my subscribers are middle aged or older; by then most of us feel we have our life pretty well figured out. But what is surprising is that after they have done a substantial amount of writing or finished their entire project, they will overwhelmingly volunteer that the best thing they got out of the writing was a clearer idea of what their life is all about! Life review is an important benefit of writing a personal history, even if it's not the reason you might undertake the project to begin with.

Writing is cathartic and healing for some people. It may function almost as psychotherapy does. It has been suggested that one of the main virtues of therapy is that it gets people to talk about their lives. Some therapists even ask their clients to write a life history. I wouldn't say call up your therapist and cancel out, but if a little writing about your life (and problems) seems to make you feel better, why not try it a little more?

Perhaps my best writing student ever was Jessie Lee Brown Foveaux at the Adult Learning Center in Manhattan, Kansas. She was also a dramatic example of the healing power of telling one's story. When I first met Jessie she was eighty years old. She came to each week's meeting with a sheaf of handwritten pages, often four or five thousand words. For much of her life, Jessie has experienced hardship and personal misfortune. Her biggest misfortune was marrying an alcoholic and abusive husband. In the 1920s, people rarely got a divorce; one married "for better or for worse." Her husband got worse and worse, and one time after he had again been arrested and jailed for drunkenness, the judge himself suggested to Jessie that she come down to his court so he could give her a divorce.

She did but felt ashamed of it. Until she began in 1978 to write about those events. She wrote her entire life story, from her girlhood in western Missouri down to the present. She had only thirty-three copies printed, one each for all her children and grandchildren. They read the book and talked about it with friends and neighbors, many of whom wrote or called Jessie to get their own copy. Reluctant at first but surprised and pleased at the positive reception, she had more books printed. By now hundreds have read her inspiring story. Subsequently, Jessie has written and self-published two more books. Now ninety-seven years old and still living in her own home, she is working on still another book. Jessie Foveaux, whom I have come to know well and am honored to have as a friend, has strengths and reserves that are amazing. I won't say that she lives on just because she has found a new role for herself as a writer, commentator, and historian, but I'm sure those interests have helped give her something to live for.

Harry Truman, as David McCullough makes clear in his massive biography of the late president, was a tireless and voluminous writer who used writing not only to communicate with others but to get things out of his system. In one seven-page "longhand spasm" (as Truman called them) written at the height of the Korean War, Truman said, "This [conflict] means all-out war. It means that Moscow, Saint Petersburg, Mukden, Vladivostock, Pekin, Shanghai, Port Arthur, Dairen, Odessa, Stalingrad, and every manufacturing plant in China and the Soviet Union will be eliminated." Had Truman ordered this in reality instead of only on paper, it would be a vastly different world today—if there would be a world at all. Instead, he chose to vent his frustration in a way that was not only harmless but healthful.

More satisfying in the long run is the development of pleasure in writing. I mean not only the pleasure of completion, of doing a parcel of good work and looking back on it, but also pleasure in the act of writing. Most writers experience some pleasure along the way, and not a few declare that their time spent writing is the happiest time of the day. The pleasure of recreating experience in words is not qualitatively different from the pleasure of doing the same thing in oil painting, for example. It is not different from the pleasure of any work, especially creative work, where things that you plan emerge, take shape, and come to have an existence apart from your own. There is also deep satisfaction in knowing that you are giving pleasure to others when they recognize the experience that you have narrated and described and say, "Yes, I remember that, too. That's just the way it was."

☞ SUGGESTION:

List your own reasons for writing family history. Use the ones listed above if you wish or any others that might be important to you. Try to list them according to importance.

Techniques for Writing Family History

Exploring Narrative Writing

In school most of us learned to do *expository writing*—otherwise known as good old English composition. It may be that you had enough of English comp. then and when you consider writing now, no matter what kind, you feel slightly ill and begin to think about all the other things you have to do. This may even make you feel a little guilty; here you've always thought about how much you'd like to write this or that family story, and now when it comes down to— shudder!—the actual writing, you remember suddenly all that stuff from English comp. and hate the idea of writing. But if you find yourself loving family stories but dreading the prospect of all that writing, you are typical. So please take heart and read on.

Writing exposition consists mostly of elaborating ideas. Exposition explains things. This book is largely expository writing. The editorial page of your newspaper is mostly exposition. The instruction booklet for your new TV, the political pamphlet tucked in your door jamb, and the article in *Reader's Digest* about violence in the streets are all examples of expository writing. Essay examinations, themes, reports, and term papers are all expository writings—that's why so much time was spent in school teaching exposition. Exposition deals basically with ideas, but narration deals basically with experience.

You might say exposition is the language of the schoolroom but narration is the language of the playground. Of course, the two forms aren't purely one or the other. That expository article about violence in the streets may have little stories in it, short narratives about kids and gangs, to illustrate the ideas that it elaborates. And the narrative history of the Oregon Trail may require a lot of exposition about the background of the people who used the trail or how the Conestoga wagon was built.

Even if you learned how to write exposition well, you probably did not learn to enjoy doing it. And since this was really the only kind of writing we commonly learned to do, it may never occur to us to write any narration. It's as if we took a course in school called Body Movement every year for twelve years that was restricted completely to doing calisthenics and heavy manual labor. So we left school not knowing that there were body movements like jogging, sports, games, and dancing, which are all relaxing and pleasurable activities. So is narrative writing.

What You Already Know About Writing Narratives

Will you now have to learn to write all over again to compose narratives? Not at all. In fact, you already know a great deal about narrating. You have been narrating stories all your life in everyday conversation. When you toddled up to your mother as a child and tearfully announced that you ate your candy and now it was "all gone," you were telling a simple story. At its simplest, a narrative is a series of actions. Later on, your narratives became more sophisticated. In the fourth grade you told your class that your family vacationed in the mountains:

> We drove all day and got to Denver, a big city, at night. We stayed in a fancy hotel there on the fifteenth floor. The next morning we had bacon and eggs for breakfast in the hotel restaurant and then we drove on to Estes Park.

This is a narrative, a series of actions, but there's more information than when you told about eating all your candy. This descriptive information helps establish a little of the scene. We get more of the picture.

Half a dozen times a day or more you narrate anecdotes of varying degrees of subtlety and sophistication. You might tell a co-worker at the office "I lost my car keys. I was late," but at home, you might tell your family:

> You know that gas station down on Eighth Street, the one we always go to, where Carol works? Well, I pulled in there, gassed up, walked over, and bought a paper and read it

while the tank was filling, then I went in and paid. Carol wasn't there, it was that other person, the guy with the frizzy hair we always thought looked like that prizefight promoter—what's his name? Anyway, when I went back to the car and got in, my keys were gone! I'm telling you, I looked high and low, in the car, out of the car, everywhere. I couldn't remember whether I took them out or not. I looked under the car, too. People were honking to get in, people stared at me like I was nuts, but I couldn't do anything but look. Finally I called the garage and they came and started it for me. But I was late, an hour late, to work.

We are not only told that a certain event took place, but we are asked to participate with the narrator in the re-creation of an event (we'll go into this crucial idea in more detail later on).

We tell stories like this all the time without thinking—you went shopping and the prices were sky-high so you drove right back home empty handed or you went to the doctor and told her about the pain in your left side but she could find nothing wrong. These are all narratives. We do this so often it's second nature; we don't even realize we're narrating. So all you have to learn about narrative writing technique is basically to transfer and build on techniques you already know from the medium of speaking, to the medium of writing.

Learning to Trust Yourself as a Writer

But what about spelling, punctuation, and the other mechanics, you may ask? Don't you need to watch your p's and q's? All of us are self-conscious about our mechanics and grammar. There's a whole industry out there of book and tape publishers who produce material based on just this fear, and none of us wants to sound stupid. My local paper runs a syndicated column every Sunday by a longtime newspaper editor and political commentator. His column is about good usage of the English language, but he does very little to dispel the common conviction that the essential thing in good writing is correctness. In his sarcastic putdowns of "mistakes" of grammar and usage, this columnist and others like him do far more to discourage people from writing than to help them become better writers. You've heard or read the motto, "Better to keep your mouth shut and be thought a fool than to open it and remove all doubt." Translate that into writing and you have a blank page.

In fact the basics of good narrative writing have to do with being specific and concrete, writing in your own authentic voice, saying exactly what you mean as simply as possible, being logical, and other similar values. Huckleberry Finn's knowledge of so-called good English is limited, yet he is one of the most articulate characters in American fiction. In one famous scene, Huck decides to go against his whole upbringing and help Jim the runaway slave escape to freedom. His "bad" English is as moving (and as elegant) as any soliloquy from *Hamlet*:

> It was awful thoughts, and awful words, but they was said. And I let them stay said; and never thought no more about reforming. . . . I would take up wickedness again, which was in my line, being brung up to it, and the other warn't. And for a starter, I would go to work and steal Jim out of slavery again; and if I could think up anything worse, I would do that, too; because as long as I was in, and in for good, I might as well go the whole hog.

Huck's sentiment was beautifully said, yet here we have the wrong pronoun being used, subjects and verbs disagreeing in number, and even the use of a nonstandard English word like *brung*. Clearly, Huck would have failed English comp.

Our real objection to what we call bad English is often social, not practical. We know very well what is meant by "He don't look crazy to me," but those of us who were brought up to speak and write "proper" English don't like the sound of it; it sounds illiterate. In short, we are snobs. This was brought home to me a couple of years ago when I wrote an article for *LifeStory* about a cookbook someone had published, and in the article I wrote that the book was bound in such a way that it "lays flat when opened." A few days after the article appeared, I received a card from a subscriber admonishing me for my bad grammar: I should have written "lies flat." Though intellectually I dismissed the card as an indicator of how obsessed some people are with grammar, I actually blushed down to the roots of my hair at my mistake. I, an English teacher, had made an elementary grammatical mistake! Was I really an English teacher or was I a fraud? At that moment I felt like the latter. And then I realized that I, too, was a language snob—perhaps more than most.

"Good" English is really the language of those people with "good" breeding. In fact, we make inferences all the time about the social class of people from their use of English. I'm not trying to suggest that we shouldn't write properly, but I am trying to suggest that writing proper English should not be so important that we refuse to write for fear of revealing our lack of education.

☛ SUGGESTION:

Is there someone in your family or community who is skilled with words but not particularly "correct" or "educated" sounding? I had a friend who was a funny, articulate, and even brilliant talker. But he had little formal education, used *ain't*, and one of his favorite comments was, "Oh, that don't make no never mind," yet he was a pleasure to listen to. Write a brief biography of an "illiterate" relative or friend of your own in which you focus on their use of language, make them talk a little, and bring forth some of their commonest expressions. This isn't a bad way of writing a biography, by the way—especially for a verbal person. If you know how such a person talks, you know a good deal about them.

Don't Try to Sound "Educated" or "Literary"

There are two other common habits of writing and speaking that are unconsciously designed to make us sound educated but that should be avoided in writing family stories. One is the habit of using the passive voice, often done out of a polite desire to hide what is really being said. Compare the active, "Someone took the car," to the passive "The car was taken."

The second habit is translating little words into big ones or using several words where one will do. The idea is to sound dignified, I suppose, but instead it clots the action of a narrative and sometimes hides it so much that it is hard to tell what is going on—or makes the reader not want to bother to find out. "It would seem to be indicated" for "It looks that way" and "I am presently employed" for "I'm working" are just a couple of simple examples. Someone who gets infected with this wordiness bug can become boring to read—or listen to. Politicians may be forgiven if they say "I am not supportive of this plan" to mean "I won't vote for this plan": they at least have a reason for speaking that way; they don't want to be understood. But if you write that way, your children will not read what you've written.

A somewhat more sophisticated form of the same impulse is

called "literariness." Some of us were taught to write in language that is "literary," as if there were such a special language that great writers used. "The sun climbed heavenward" for "The sun came up" is a simple example. But such writing is ineffective; it doesn't do the job. No one talks that way. It only expresses the poetic education of the writer, and calls attention to that.

Remember that the members of your family and your close friends are going to be your readers. They want you to sound like you, just as if you were sitting in your living room talking to them. They will be disappointed if you sound like a professional writer addressing the literary public. Even if you are a writer with a good deal of experience (as budding family historians often are), your family want you to sound intimate and real, not journalistic or literary or academic. There is skill involved in learning to relax and be yourself in writing, and that's some of what this book is about. There are other skills that you already have in considerable supply, however, skills that you can build on. To learn to be authentically yourself sounds like a contradiction in terms. Why would you have to learn to be what you already are? But to learn to avoid sounding like a schoolroom writer—to unlearn how to write, if you like to look at it that way—means going into your project with some consciousness of the possible pitfalls and with your eyes wide open. Generally, the best defense against not being authentic is to read your own work aloud to yourself. Listen carefully to how you sound. If you sound like you do when you are relaxed and in an informal setting, then you're probably on target.

What I am asking you to do at this point is not so much develop new skills but develop new attitudes. With training, skills develop. New attitudes are more elusive. It will take some thought. You won't change all the ideas you have about writing with a snap of your fingers. You may intellectually agree immediately, but developing new attitudes will take awareness and time.

☛ SUGGESTION:

Write out a story you've told today or quite recently in exactly (as best you can recall) the words you used to tell it. This may be a simple story only a few lines long. Your story may have involved some exposition (explanation) and may have involved some conversation. Put it all in, just as you told it. Don't upgrade your language or style. Strive to write it just as you told it.

Getting Started Writing

By now I hope you've taken some of the suggestions offered and started writing. If you haven't, start now. The rest of the reading will make far more sense if you are already writing. Use some of the suggestions or go off on your own. The essential thing is to start. Suppose you find yourself sitting at your writing desk with your chin resting on your folded hands thinking thoughts like, "Maybe I'll write about the time Dad and I went fishing in Ontario. But how will I start? Well, maybe Ontario isn't such a hot idea. What about a story of Dad at work, seeing patients? Nahh. That sounds boring. Perhaps Dad and Mom together at the dinner table. Dad used to tease Mom about her cooking, but what's that matter? Oh, well, I wonder what's on TV?"

If wondering what to write about is happening to you, reach up and turn on the red emergency light and write about the first thing that comes to mind. Get a handful of family photos and begin writing with the very first one. Writing photo captions of a few lines or so is a good way to get moving. Very often, writing any sketch or anecdote or story doesn't seem interesting or exciting until you are deeply into it. Do the writing, get involved in the story, and don't worry about being excited. I guarantee that narrative writing is fun, but getting started can be a lot like work.

Making lists is a form of writing. Taking notes of any sort is a form of writing. Both of these activities are legitimate and helpful ways for a writer to start work. Supposing you are sitting, trying to think of how to write about what your father told you of his youth. Start writing a list now using your journal. Here is one I put together for my father:

1. Went fishing in pasture trout streams.
2. Was a lone scout, went camping all by himself with fishhooks and hatchet.
3. Didn't date until college.
4. Studied hard, got A's.
5. Once participated in a Hallowe'en prank putting a board across a sidewalk and an old lady tripped and fell and broke her nose.
6. Lettered in every sport in high school.

Too many family histories never get written because the would-be writer wastes time staring off into space thinking vaguely about organization or what approach to take. The list called for in the following suggestion is one excellent way to organize a life story.

☞ SUGGESTION:

Think of yourself as the director of a film about your life. List at least ten scenes from your life that you would want to include in your movie. Briefly describe them:

1. I am in first grade and reciting in class
2. My granddad holds me on his lap and sings to me
3. I get a job delivering the paper in my neighborhood.

Keep this list at your writing desk, and when (and if) you "block" pull up one of these scenes and begin to make notes about it. For instance, you might write the following for item 3.

Mr. Grimshaw's dog scares me to death every day and chases me down the street.

Mrs. Gonzales always gives me a cookie.

I come home with ink on my hands.

In bad weather Dad would sometimes take me in the car to deliver the papers.

If your notes stir you up enough that you go ahead and write up the scene, do so, of course. Otherwise, leave it until later. If you are beginning your writing of family history with a biography of a parent or other ancestor, do the same thing and make a list of scenes from their life.

Writing as a Way of Remembering

Sometimes people are reluctant to start writing because they can't remember something. They will sit in a chair or do chores while they try to remember. Maybe a woman wants to remember something of her girlhood back in Oklahoma but has only a few images in her mind of that time. It's a shame we can't remember everything we want to when we want to. But remembering can be an active process.

Though memories do sometimes just pop into your head as you're walking along, the simple act of writing can make memories come.

But how, you might ask, can you sit down to write about something you don't even remember? You proceed on faith. While you may remember only a little, it helps to write, "I don't remember that guy's name in Cleveland in 1956," or "All I remember of those years in Texas is an image of my father kissing Mom good-bye and going off to work." It's a bit of a paradox to try to write about something that you don't remember, but a single image can lead to another image, then to another, and so on.

In the passage below from my own life, I go back to a time that I have some memories of and would certainly want to include in my autobiography: my life swimming and playing in the "crick." You'll have to trust me when I tell you that this is the first and only time I've written this and that I've changed nothing for its inclusion here. My point is to demonstrate how much you remember when you actively try to write about a specific time of your life.

My Life in the Crick

From 1947 to the late summer of 1951 we lived on a farm six miles out of town with a creek running through it. It was a sizable creek that began a few miles west of our farm and flowed into the Kansas River a few miles further east. It was big enough to have a name, Deep Creek.

In fact it was fairly deep, deep enough that there were several good swimming holes in the half mile or so of it that belonged to us because it ran across our farm.

I remember once my brother said he'd give me a quarter if I'd walk naked from our favorite swimming hole up the open road to the windmill. The swimming hole was the one with the log sticking up out of it that we always used as a diving board, I remember how slippery with moss it was underneath the water, but always as dry as toast outside of it. That log was a perfect diving board.

I told my brother I'd do it. We always swam naked. We knew about swimming suits, but none of the farm boys we knew wore one. It would have been considered sissified here on the farm. In town, of course, people went swimming in concrete pools and had to wear a suit. But of course we didn't walk down to the creek naked. We wore clothes and dropped them in a heap on the bank. To walk naked now to the windmill through several hundred yards of open country, even though there weren't any other farmhouses close by, was a bit of a dare. I took it. I guess I needed the quarter.

I made the walk. It was a sunny, breezy day. I didn't ordinarily go barefoot except when swimming. Maybe I remember the hot dusty road, how I had to step along to keep my feet from getting burned. Maybe I walked along the edge some in the grass, or down the middle where no tires rolled and so grass grew, and it was cooler.

I got back to the swimming hole and demanded my quarter. My brother gravely walked over to his pants and took a piece of paper from his pocket. He tore it into four pieces and handed me my "quarter."

This memory of my brother's joke, except for some of the specifics like the moss on the log, is old, but writing this memory made other memories come flooding back, recollections of things I'd long thought I'd forgotten: how I got in the habit of smoking by using cigarettes to burn leeches off my legs after hours of playing in the creek, how we even went swimming when the creek was flooding and the water was swirling and brown, how we camped along the creek one night and the water came up in heavy rains and took the food we had stored in a bucket sitting in the water, how my father used to go swimming with us sometimes after he got home from work, and how Mom was the only one who wore a suit. Her suit was a one-piece red affair that was sort of like a modern miniskirt that she wore with a rubber bathing cap, though I don't think she did anything more than wade up to her ankles. Dad got in and paddled around and even taught us the name "dog paddling" for the kind of swimming style we all used. He might have also taught us the breast stroke and the Australian crawl. He looked funny with his glasses off, paddling around. I even remember how the water in the deep parts felt so freezing cold on our lower legs and feet and that the fish would nibble on our toes if we held still for a few seconds. Now I recall the high banks at one end of the swimming hole, and the bend and then a shallow rapids part and how we'd go to the rapids at the other end and make dams and channels and sometimes fool around almost all day long.

This is probably enough to demonstrate my point. In the process of writing up the vivid memory of my brother's joke on me, which I haven't thought of in a long time, I have jarred loose numerous other memories and physical details long forgotten. Any one or two of these could be the basis for an anecdote about this particular time of my own youth. I have no doubt these images and writing this anecdote will lead to other memories. This technique is invaluable in allowing you to almost enter into the past again, to feel things, to smell and see and hear as you did then. Try it. Think of it as taking notes or as writing your stream of consciousness. This kind of "automatic writing" where you don't try to direct yourself with your conscious mind is a great way to start out writing about a period of your life. Think of it as spade work.

☞ SUGGESTION:

Write about ten minutes of the stream of your consciousness. Make no effort to punctuate or even make sense, just describe what's going on in your mind for these few minutes. Think of yourself as your mind's secretary, taking dictation.

Conversation helps stimulate memories, too. This is why old friends and family love to talk about the old days—one memory leads to another. You may want to tape some of these conversations, play them later, and then do some automatic writing immediately following.

Visiting old friends, even going back to the places you lived, can be extremely helpful. A couple of years ago I visited the village in Indiana where I had lived as a small child during World War II. I looked for the general store where I used to buy barlow knives and fishhooks, but the only thing left was a foundation. An old man walking by told me the place had burned to the ground thirty years before. Even so, being there stimulated my memory so much that I sat in my car for a solid hour writing as fast as I could, recalling many images.

There are other simple devices to stimulate your memory: drawing a floor plan to remember your house, a map of your farm or the town where you lived, or even the face of a parent or other close relative. You don't have to be an artist or worry about drawing a good likeness. You may be like me and be an incompetent artist, but the act of drawing will cause memories to come full blown into your head that you didn't know you had.

You will not be able to remember everything, obviously, and some things you think you remember may be from another period.

Your memory may actually be a composite. Or you may engage in "retrospective fabrication," restructuring past memories to fit your interpretation of your past. That your memory will be selective and imperfect is simply human. Don't let its occasional fallibility stop you from using it because you do remember much, much more than you think you do. It's all there in your mind just waiting for you to come along and write it down.

☞ SUGGESTION:

Draw a floor plan of the house you lived in as a child. If you lived in a house with several stories, go ahead and draw each floor. Label each room "my bedroom," "kitchen," "Mom and Dad's room," and so on. Put in any details about the rooms you recall now—where the stove was, a bookshelf, the easy chairs—and in the margins make some notes about the memories that the act of drawing brings back. These are notes to yourself so don't worry about complete sentences, but do make the notes clear enough for others to read. Put in any memories that come to mind. "This is the chair Mom sat in evenings, where in the light of a floor lamp she darned socks and knitted."

The Importance of Being Specific

If you think about your friends and family who are the best storytellers, the ones whose words everyone hangs on, you will find their stories are specific. They don't say things like, "I had an awful day at work today," or if they do, they don't let the story go at that. They'll go on to say why they had an awful day:

> First, the mail was two hours late. When old Williams, the postman, came in finally at eleven, his face was sagging almost as much as his big leather pouch. He said to me, "I never saw so much junk mail as I did in my cart this morning."

Such storytellers go on telling the story until they're done, because they've discovered somewhere along the line that if people are going to listen they are going to have to be specific. It's the same way with reading, only more so. Where a talker can to some extent insist on the listener hearing the story, a reader has to depend on being interesting from the first word. It's easy enough to get into the habit of being specific. A good way to practice is when speaking. For example, here are some opening lines that probably won't generate much enthusiasm:

1. It's a beautiful day.
2. The kids were lots of fun today.
3. Traffic was heavy on the way home.
4. Everyone was very friendly at work today.
5. The crowd at the airport was very interesting.

Ask the questions that might occur normally after hearing these sentences and then recast the opening line to answer those questions. What's beautiful about the day? "What a morning! Did you see the flowers in Roosevelt Park?" Why were the kids fun? "Justin and Sarah kept me laughing all morning with their play." Then go on to tell specifically what they did that made you laugh—if their play was antic, how was it antic?

Consider these revisions of opening lines three, four, and five:

"It took twenty minutes to get through the lights all along Vandervent Boulevard. All the drivers were glaring at each other."

"When I got to work Carol and the others whipped out a cake and sang 'Happy Birthday.' "

"Watching the crowd at the airport was like watching people get off Noah's Ark—there were people from every nation on earth, speaking a dozen different languages, wearing Indian clothes, African clothes—or they were just Americans dressed in all kinds of ways from formal evening clothes to hippies in cutoffs and bandannas around their forehead."

You'll find also that the more specific you are, the less you have to think about what to write next. When I was a classroom teacher, I would ask students to write about "life." I'd write the word in big letters on the blackboard and they would stare at it. No one would start writing. Then under that I'd write "college life," and suggest they write about that. They'd shift in their seats and one or two would smile and start to write. Then I'd write under those words the phrase "college social life," and even more would take off, and by the time I got down to asking them to write about the social life of their own dormitory, they all had ideas and were up and running. *Life* is too general a term to suggest much of anything, but nothing is more specific (and real) to you than your own life right in front of you. The more specific you can be, the more interesting you'll be, the more fun you'll have, and the more you'll have to say.

One of the nicest things about writing when compared with talking, by the way, is that no one will interrupt you. You can go into as much detail as you like.

Engage the Reader's Senses

When you write, think of creating a scene or picture so that readers can see in their minds what it was like to be there. A good storyteller makes readers feel like they are there experiencing the story and not merely being told about events. To a large degree this is a matter of being specific and writing *physically*.

Consider how the process of reading and writing works. You as the writer form images in your mind of a family picnic long ago, of children threading in and out of clusters of adults standing and talking and eating. You see various specific images as if you were looking at photographs stored all these years in your head. Then you search for words to express these images and you write them down on paper. If you choose your words well, words that convey images to the reader, then the reader will imagine something like the experience you had in reality so many years ago.

Now it's amazing that we not only have physical senses, but also can *imagine* these sensations. We can imagine a stinky smell or a screeching sound. We've all had the experience of having someone describe something disgusting at the dinner table so that we lose our appetite—or the experience of reading about a delicious meal so that we get out of bed at three o'clock in the morning and raid the refrigerator. We don't have to actually experience hunger to become hungry—that's one of the premises that makes stories so interesting. We can *virtually* experience things.

In response to a request to write physically and concretely, Sandra Gregersen wrote the following memoir about her farm girlhood. As you read this piece—and note by the way that she doesn't just write about "farm life" but about "coming home from school and going out to the barn to help Dad with the cows"—consider the physical sensations you experience in your mind. Some of them are so intense that you may actually find yourself reacting physically too. I have read this short slice of life to dozens of groups and their reaction has been uniformly one of pleasure. As you read, consider why.

Barn Chores
by Sandra Gregersen

A blast of pungent, steamy air hit me in the face as I opened the door to help with afternoon chores. It smelled of cow manure and hay dust mingled with corn silage and ground feed.

The barn was the center of all outdoor activities during the winter months. It was a friendly, cozy place with ten Holsteins, the horse, the dog, numerous cats of all sizes, and a few chickens.

The barn was new, built of cement blocks by my dad in 1952. It was warm and comfortable inside, even though the walls were covered with frost from the animals' body heat.

At twelve, I actually liked to help Dad with barn chores. I liked it better than setting the table or washing dishes. So after school I changed into my everyday jeans and sweat-shirt, put on my zipper overshoes and well-worn jacket, and hurried to the barn, while my sister stayed in the house to help Mom.

Teddy, our dog, was the first to hear me as I entered the barn. He jumped up to lick my face, and almost knocked me down he was so happy to see me. Babe nickered from her stall in the corner, and the cats ran out from their hiding place between the straw bales. Dad was already pumping fresh water on top of the ice in the stock tank, the begin-ning of his twice-daily routine.

He asked me about school as the tank filled. I talked and he listened. At my feet four pesky cats clamored for atten-tion. One of the kittens climbed up my pants leg to get at my after-school treat of freshly baked chocolate cake. I shared some crumbs with each cat and Teddy, and kept the frosting for myself.

"Well, the sooner we get started, the sooner we'll be done," Dad said.

My job was to let the cows and the horse outside for wa-ter. I walked down the line in front of the cows, releasing each cow from her stanchion. If a stanchion lever stuck, I wasn't strong enough to get the cow's head free. Then Dad stopped what he was doing and came over to help me.

The cow, impatient to get outside for water, would pull her head back tight against the stanchion. Dad would slap the cow's rump and she would step ahead so he could release the lever. Sometimes a cow would relieve herself as she went down the walkway out the door. I pinched my nose and wrinkled my face in disgust as the manure splattered on the cement. Dad took his shovel and quickly cleaned the walkway so the next cow wouldn't slip.

When all the cows were outside, I unhooked Babe's halter snap and led her to the door. She ran after the cows like a kid at recess, galloping and romping in the yard. I closed the door, and we hurried with the chores. Without the animals, the barn was cold.

Dad shoveled the manure from the gutter into a wheelbarrow. Then he wheeled it outside to the ever-increasing pile in the cow yard. All winter the manure pile grew bigger and bigger until spring when Dad could spread it on the corn field.

While Dad cleaned the gutter, I freshened the bedding, mounding the straw where each cow lay for the night. With a pitchfork I shook the old straw and added a new bale. If I raised too much dust, I coughed and blew dirt out my nose.

Next I spread a bale of hay in the feed bunk and divided it equally among the ten stanchions. Stopping to rest, I played cat and mouse with the kittens in the hay. Cats were always underfoot vying for attention. "They've got to learn to stay out of the way or the cows will step on them when they come back in," Dad warned, and started to carry out the corn silage to the feed bunk.

Each cow received a big scoop of the steamy silage. The smell was awful. I wondered how a cow could possibly eat it, as I compared it with sauerkraut, only worse. I followed along behind Dad with a pail of ground corn and sprinkled a handful on top of each scoop of silage. I thought of it as topping for the dessert.

By this time some of the cows, finished at the stock tank, were waiting to come back into the barn. In anticipation of the feed in their bunk, they bunched by the door, pushing and shoving each other to be first inside when the door opened.

As I completed brooming the walkway, Dad said, "Stand back now so the cows don't spook when they see you. If they get nervous they won't come in to the right stanchions."

I knew that each cow had her own place. If a cow did get

in the wrong stanchion, Dad would have to back her out and move her along to the right spot. From the tone of his voice, I knew it was not something I wanted to cause.

Dad opened the barn door and I crouched down with the cats out of sight. I heard the cows tramping on the cement, clanging into the stanchions and snorting ground feed from their nostrils. I peeked around the corner. Dad yelled at a cow, "Get out of there!"

The cow, reluctant to move, grabbed a big slobbering mouthful of ground feed before going to her own stanchion. When the cows were all settled, Dad walked down the line, snapped the stanchion levers, and locked each cow in place.

Finished, he walked over to me, put his hand on my shoulder, and said, "Let's go eat."

☞ SUGGESTION:

Pick an area of your past or present life that seems to you to be especially sensory, really loaded with smells, sounds, and sights. Narrate a few minutes from such a time, just as Sandra has done above in "Barn Chores." It might be that one sense is more prevalent in your selection than another. That's okay, but whether it's one sense you remember or many, lay it on thick: think of yourself trying to make the reader experience the senses that you did when this bit of your history took place.

Mixing Summary and Scene

A narrative is a series of actions taking place over a period of time. Since you cannot and wouldn't want to recreate every single scene from your history in narrating a given event, you start making choices about what to tell and what to leave out. You do this naturally and without much thought when you are telling a story out loud. When you write the story, however, you may want to make some notes beforehand. It's very useful to think of your story as a series of scenes. Some scenes will be very important and fully developed, others will be developed only slightly, and others may not really need to be scenes at all but may be summarized.

The deciding factor is always what your story is about, a process called focusing your narrative. The focus of your narrative determines what to summarize and what to present as scene. For example, suppose you narrate the story of your skiing vacation in Aspen.

Very quickly you summarize how you got on a plane, flew to Aspen, rode on a shuttle to the lodge, donned your skis, and hiked to the slopes. Then you slow down and present the scene—the beautiful sunny day, the quality of the sparkling snow, the skis, your friends' comments, and so on. Where you took perhaps four lines to travel a thousand miles to get there, you now take a hundred lines to elaborate on skiing down a slope of less than a thousand feet! But it's quite natural to do that because skiing—not an airplane trip—is what your story is about. Skiing is your focus.

Keeping this focus in mind will naturally guide you into knowing what to present as scene and what to summarize. One excellent way to keep your focus sharp is to give your story a title before you begin. A title that is descriptive and a statement of the story's point works very well to keep both reader and writer on track. The following narrative is from my own life. I've put the summary in italics.

The Summer I Became a Forger

The summer I was fifteen my brother and I moved to Milwaukee and started looking for jobs. We made the rounds, but we soon realized something was wrong. The city was in the grips of an economic crisis. The breweries, which employed thousands of Milwaukeans, were out on strike and had been for several months. Most of the jobs that normally would have gone to young and inexperienced people like my brother and me were taken by strikers who were earning some money on the side to supplement their strike fund benefits. Still, I persevered and finally landed a job as a messenger boy in a large printing plant downtown.

"You will need a work permit," the man who hired me said. "Do you have one?"

"A work permit?" I didn't know what he meant.

He explained that in Wisconsin everyone had to have a permit to work, issued by the State Industrial Commission. Because I was young, I would have to show proof that I was at least sixteen. No one in Wisconsin could work in a business or factory unless they were at least sixteen.

"You are sixteen, aren't you?" he asked.

"Oh, yes, sir," I lied. The truth was I was barely fifteen.

I told him I'd get the necessary permit and come back the next day. But I went home in despair. How was I going to get a work permit when I wasn't old enough?

With the help of my big brother, we cooked up a scheme. I actually had my birth certificate in my possession, and so we carefully erased the last digit in the year of my birth. Then we went to a library and rented a typewriter with similar pica type and typed in a seven where an eight had been. Voilà, I was a year older!

But the lady at the Industrial Commission was suspicious. "This looks like it's been erased," she said. She reached in her desk and took out a magnifying glass and studied it. She even showed me. "See? It looks a little rough there," she said. She wasn't a mean lady. She was just doing her job.

"Well, I didn't erase anything," I said.

"Still, it looks doctored, and so we will not accept this as proof of your age."

Summary and scene are mixed in narrative all the time, and you should feel free to move back and forth from one to the other. Sometimes, of course, you will want to only imply that something happened—it will be so unimportant or so obvious that you won't need even to summarize it. Suppose you are telling about your sophomore year in school that was marked by the first day when you met a cute girl and then the developing relationship you had with her the whole year. Maybe classes were pretty much a blur. You don't need to tell about them at all except to mention that you were in school. Your narrative might be marked by phrases like, "After history class, Sally and I held hands in the hall and stared into each other's eyes. . . . After school, we went downtown for a Coke." Kurt Vonnegut once said that in his novels no one ever opens a car door. What he meant was he narrated only what was important to the focus of his narrative.

Sometimes inexperienced writers begin a story by summarizing what they are about to present as scene: "In the old days we didn't swim in concrete pools but in 'the old swimmin' hole' in the creek that ran across our place. Most of the time we wore nothing but our birthday suits. Our diving board was a log or a rope tied to an overhanging tree . . ." and so the writer might go on and on, explaining what he is about to present all over again but much more dramatically when he gets into the tale of how he and his best friend, Buck, would spend entire days playing in the creek. The summary simply steals the dramatic thunder from the narrative to follow. You'll be amazed at how much readers appreciate your assuming they have the intelligence to figure some things out for themselves. For example, that same opening sentence might be rewritten this way: "Buck grabbed the rope and swung high out over the water, yelling down to all of us as he dropped: 'Geronimo!' " We know where Buck is, and we know what he's doing.

Starting in the middle of things is an effective way to draw the reader in. The reader is involved and engaged, and then when you give information about the creek or what you did or didn't wear and so on, it can be sprinkled in naturally as the narrative moves along. The reader is more apt to pay attention then, too.

Summary works best to establish a scene, to provide continuity from one scene to the next, or to tell about something that the reader may need to know but for one reason or another is not the focus of your narrative.

It's a danger sign, though, if you find yourself summarizing without doing much in the way of scene. Summary by itself is boring. Consider this, if you can stay awake:

> That summer was just great. We played all kinds of games and went swimming a lot. I had lots of friends and went lots of places with them. On Sundays, we drove to towns all around our own and visited relatives. Then during the week I helped Mom around the house when I wasn't playing. School started again in the fall.

This is a summary crying to be one or two scenes. A single scene at the swimming pool, visiting a family of cousins and aunts and uncles in a single town, or even helping Mom with the chores would be interesting and, more to the point, informative. It would make us feel the story as an experience.

It may sometimes be necessary to stop the narrative and explain something in order for the narrative to be understood. Then exposition is just the thing. If you're narrating a story about a toy your grandfather made for you that isn't like any toy your readers are likely to know about, you will want to stop and describe it and explain how it worked. Do that just as naturally as you would if you were telling the story to friends, then get back to the narrative.

☞ SUGGESTION:

Think of any story you are contemplating writing as a series of scenes. Put those scenes that you want to develop in capital letters; put the ones you can simply summarize in small letters.

Writing a Composite Scene

Sometimes it's desirable to write a scene that in reality never took place as a single event. Instead, pieces are spliced together from several scenes, creating a composite scene. For dramatic purposes composite scenes are presented as if they were one scene. Suppose, for example, you wanted to convey what your life was like when you were a sailor on board ship. Let's say that you were a sailor five years, and that time was characterized by standing watches, reading, playing cards, shooting the bull in the day room, drinking vast quantities of coffee, and standing against the ship's rail and watching the ship being maneuvered into her berth in port.

These events are typical and humdrum so you're not likely to remember a specific day when you did all of these things, and even if you did the reader would not want to read about the number of incidents that you'd need to write to make your points about your life as a sailor. One composite scene can do the job. For the purposes of getting your history across, it is perfectly all right to make one up just as long as you're true to the important facts. Historians do this all the time. You might even present it as a typical day:

> Most mornings I got up at six and ate a big breakfast of sausage and eggs that I washed down with a mug or two of hot coffee. I'd get a refill from Cooky and then go into the Day Room where I'd have a smoke and sip the coffee until it was time to go on watch. I'd shoot the bull with other members of the Deck Department, often the bo'sun Ted Hartner, who like me had grown up in the Midwest. Ted was a lot older, and had been to sea for many years. He had rough red hands and a big happy face that wouldn't have looked out of place on a Nebraska farmer sitting on a tractor. He once told me that maneuvering a ship into a berth wasn't a whole lot different from getting a team of mules to the field hitched up to a plow. "Generally, the ship is more cooperative," he said. Then he'd laugh. I liked him and respected his knowledge.
>
> "Where's a good place to have fun in Istanbul?" I'd ask him if we were in the Mediterranean hopping from port to port.
>
> "Fun for a guy your age or a guy my age?" Ted said. "If I go ashore at all in Istanbul I go to this little tea room on the

dock and sip tea and practice speaking Turkish with the waiters."

Some trips I'd go with Ted, save my money, have a pleasant time, and get a good night's sleep before we'd get underway next morning. That was when I had a really busy watch, hustling from hawser to hawser.

This composite allows you to show something of your leisure routine, a little bit about at least one of your companions in those days, as well as something about your work routine. A composite scene may not have the sustained sense of reality that an ordinary scene has—you may have to show your hand a little more often and lead the reader around ("Today was smooth sailing and I didn't have much to do but repair lines, but when we were pitching and rolling in bad weather the Chief had me running"), but the advantage of covering a lot of territory in a single scene is probably worth it.

Telling Narratives from a Specific Point of View

A scene, even an entire history, is told from a point of view. Usually, this point of view will be your own. You, the narrator, are also the author. Your vision as you move around in the story will be limited to what you can see, which is less confusing and heightens the sense of reality for the reader. If you are writing about doing household chores on Saturdays when you lived at home with your parents, brothers, and sisters, it's much easier on the reader—and you too—if you stay with your own point of view. Perhaps you are doing the ironing and you can describe how the iron was heated on the stove. You might want to describe the other chores too—dusting the furniture, doing the wash, making beds, and so on, and maybe your brothers and sisters are doing these chores. But it's generally simpler to tell it all as if you were either doing it or watching them do it so that it's all filtered through you. Otherwise the reader is going to feel like several different people are trying to talk to him all at once.

There are exceptions. One might be in a biography of an ancestor. This ancestor has come and gone and you are in a position to know much more about some things than she did. You may know, for example, how she died and where. You may know that her children grew to adulthood and filled up an entire town, prospered, grew old, and died. But for dramatic purposes, in order to make the experience you are presenting seem more realistic, you may wish to tell her story as if the narrator didn't know all those things. Then you will tell the story from her point of view and will be limited most of the time by what she sees and does. You may find it necessary for one reason or another to step out of her point of view occasionally, but remember that every time you do you undermine her reality as a character and make your narrative a little bit less dramatic, just as seeing the hands of the puppetmaster makes the audience believe a lot less in the reality of the puppets' story.

Another exception occurs when you want to take advantage of the superior believability of first-person point of view, and so you might want to pretend in a biography of your grandmother that you are she, that the "I" of your story is your grandmother speaking. This can be very dramatic. It can also give you (and your readers) insight into what it was like to be that person. You may need to invent a good deal to make it credible, and that's okay too as long as the invention (a) is pointed out to be such, (b) is true to the basic facts of the story, and (c) is something that, if it did not happen, might or even should have.

If by now you are getting the feeling that the greatest challenge you face in writing history is making your readers believe you, then you are right. Meeting this challenge is also the most fun. This is the art of writing family history, but like any art it consists of specific learned skills as well as talent. What you have going for you is that you are already quite experienced at these skills—all you have to do is make the transfer from speaking to writing.

Making a Person Real with Words

History is mostly biography, and a biography is made of words. These words will convey what your subject (which could of course be you) is like to the reader. You want the reader to feel the presence of this person. Once again you have a lot to build on. You've been talking about other people all your life, and that's really all you'll be doing when you do family history. Here are some common ways to make your subject come to life.

1. Describe briefly their physical reality: their looks, manner-isms, and overall impression on you and others. Precise weights and heights aren't especially useful, unless your subject was of unusual di-mensions. But glimpses can bring them to life:

> Grandma wore her hair in a bun. It was thick and snow white, and when occasionally I'd see her with it down be-low her shoulders it was stunning. She scowled at me a great deal—I always seemed to be getting in trouble, sleep-ing late or skipping out to go swimming—and she would shake her head and cluck her tongue.

2. One of the best means of characterizing somebody is hav-ing them speak. This is such an important trait of a good biography that I've devoted a whole section later to the topic. It's enough to say here that you should give some thought to and make some notes about how any of the people you're writing about (including your-self, of course) use language. It's one of the fundamental ways we define who we are. Ironically, even people who aren't talkative are often characterized by their language use: "He is a man of few words." Reproduce some of your subject's speech mannerisms, ways, and common phrases: " 'You boys,' Grandma would say to us at the table when we wouldn't eat our food. 'You eat like birds. You'll never grow up.' "

3. Show their actions in little, everyday things. Were they likely to pet a dog or push it away? My grandmother never stopped tidying up. She'd stop in the parlor and fluff up a pillow or straighten up a crooked pile of magazines. She always seemed to have a dust-cloth at hand to wipe a bit of imaginary (to me) dust off a shelf edge or the top of the radio knobs.

4. Don't leave out larger, characteristic actions. To continue with my grandmother as an example, I recall that she made her own bread, and when it was hot out of the oven she'd give us kids a big slice with some homemade jam. When the neighborhood kids came too, she'd give them slices as well but complain later. One day I no-ticed that if the neighbor kids did not come, she'd arrange some kind of excuse to get them over so she could feed them. When she watched us kids eating what she had made for us, she smiled broadly.

5. Letters are an important source for biographers. When the habit (or maybe it was just necessity) of writing and saving letters

was popular, it was often possible to almost reconstruct someone's life based on their letters. People don't resort to letters as much today (though the rise of electronic mail is encouraging), but for the older generation who not only wrote letters but saved them, letters will be a great source of all kinds of information about the subject's thoughts and actions. Naturally, if your subject kept a diary or journal that you have access to, these would also be just as important. A person writing to himself is likely to sound different when writing to someone else. Letters may give one impression, and a diary might add another. Don't overlook any possible material in order to establish the character of your subject. When you form certain opinions about your subject as a result of reading letters and journals, be sure to quote from those sources to fortify your opinions.

> Arthur loved to fly. In a letter to his sister, he wrote, "I hope you'll take me along the next time you fly. I love it and can think of no better way to get to China."

6. What others think about your subject will be important too. Sometimes several different interviews may elicit several different opinions. This doesn't necessarily mean anyone's mistaken or lying: it's quite possible that Uncle Bill seemed friendly and outgoing to one person and quiet and withdrawn with someone else. This may only mean that Uncle Bill was a complex person.

Re-creating Conversations

Strangely, one narrative skill that is seldom put to use in writing family history is reproducing conversation or dialogue. This is a shame. Conversation is a big part of our lives. So why doesn't it show up in family histories? One reason, I think, is that in spite of all the minutiae of handling the written language we were subjected to in school, we were given little or no instruction and even less practice in writing dialogue. Even the mechanics of it seem abstruse and confusing to us. Yet the mechanics are not so important in real life. The usual practice is to use quotation marks (what one family writer called "wasps" because of their resemblance to that insect), but some writers introduce speech in narrative with a dash (—) and not much more; it's also easy to follow. Mark speech the way that seems easiest for you. A second reason people sometimes do not use conversation in their family histories arises out of a well intended but unnecessarily literal regard for factual history. I have had many people tell me they haven't written conversations in their life story because they can't remember the exact words. And this goes double for those writing about people whose conversations they were not privy to at all.

But the fact is that historians and biographers make up conversations all the time for dramatic purposes. This is perfectly ethical as long as the conversations might have happened or are reconstructions that are true to the facts. Dwight D. Eisenhower, in a preface to a collection of narratives about his life called *At Ease*, begins with this disclaimer:

> I am usually opposed to the author who puts within quotation marks conversations he never heard or who pretends to recollect with absolute fidelity conversations he heard a long time ago. Now, there are a few conversations reported in this book in which I did not take part and others, which I did hear at first hand, that took place fifty or even seventy or more years ago. Of the latter, the key phrases are indelibly imprinted in my memory. But I have engaged in some reconstruction. Consequently I urge the reader to take all the quoted material, particularly that recollected across the decades, with the necessary grain of salt.

Dramatizing isn't the only reason for including conversations in your work. Ease of reading is another. Most readers shy away from solid pages of wall to wall text. Conversation helps break this up, and of course speech is livelier too because in a sense it is action—the act of people talking.

Maybe the most important reason for including conversation in a family history is that it's a great way to characterize people. What someone says and how that person says it provide excellent insights into character. "What kind of guy is he?" we might ask, and nod with understanding when we are told he is "chatty," "forthcoming," or "talkative." How people look may not matter and how they think may be beyond our ken, but how they talk is something we know about and pay attention to. It's almost the first thing we notice. Does she talk slowly and deliberately or does she jabber nervously? Does he mumble and mutter or is he direct and blunt?

Many traits of speaking can be shown in conversations. They may be the best way, in fact, to show what your people are really like. All you have to do is put them into the scene and start them talking something like the way they really talked. Writers who do this very well are said to have an "ear" for dialogue, but this isn't something they were born with. We are all more or less able to have an ear, and it is just a matter of making sure it shows in the writing. As with other narrative writing skills, it can be developed with a little practice. It's a lot of fun, really.

Now for some tips for writing conversation.

✻ **Make it easy for the reader to know who's speaking.** Start a new paragraph every time you change speakers. It's for your reader's benefit, and helps avoid confusion about who's speaking. For example,

"Where's your mother?" Dad asked.

"I think she's in the kitchen," I said.

"No, she isn't. I just looked."

"Oh," I said. "Maybe she's out in the garden then."

"I'll check," Dad said.

✻ **Avoid long speeches.** Break up a long speech by reference to the other actions that are going on during it. We don't stand still and make speeches to one another. Consider the following passage:

The boss said, "Maybe you'd like to be promoted. Everyone needs one now and then. You've been on the order desk now for . . . let's see . . . thirteen years. Maybe you'd like to move up to management? I could use someone there with your experience. The pay's better, too."

Now read this version for a heightened sense of reality:

"Maybe you'd like to be promoted," the boss said to Dad. "Everybody needs one now and then." He smiled at my father.

Dad leaned back in his chair and returned Mr. Dithers' smile.

"You've been on the order desk now for . . . let's see . . . thirteen years, isn't it?

Dad nodded. He watched Dithers roll the paper he was holding in his hand and then unroll it again.

"Maybe you'd like to move up to management," Mr. Dithers said, not exactly as a question, but more as if he were talking to himself or thinking out loud.

Dad's smiled broadened into a grin. He couldn't think of a thing to say.

"The pay's better, too," Dithers added.

"I thought you'd never ask," Dad finally said, and the two men laughed.

❋ **Use simple labels.** Use speech tags like *he said* or *she said* after the speech or in between parts of it if they are necessary to show who's speaking. It's okay, sometimes, to put tags at the beginning, as in, He said, "I am going to work," but don't overdo it. Use adverbs sparingly. Instead of *He said coldly* or *She said flippantly*, have the actual speaking show the coldness and the flippancy. The rule of narrative writing is Show, don't tell. This isn't always possible, but in general it's a good practice. And avoid phrases like *She assented, He avowed*, and so on for the same reason—the assenting or the avowal should be shown in the conversation. Also, the attempt to avoid using the same word over and over shows up far more conspicuously than the simple *said*.

❋ **Acknowledge paraphrasing.** Remembering conversations word for word is not necessary except where everything hinges on precise wording, as when words might have been chosen very carefully. If at some point exact words are important and you can't remember them, intercede yourself into the narrative or put in a footnote and frankly state that you have your doubts.

> I can't remember Uncle Bill's exact words then. I've asked others in the family who were there and their recollection is very, very similar to mine. "I'll sell the whole farm or none of it," he said, or words to that effect.

Do the best you can to remember, but the important thing is to pay attention to the tone of the conversation and to the speech habits of everyone involved. If you're writing about your father and he had favorite stock phrases like "Don't take any wooden nickels" or "See you later, alligator," use them. The idea is to convey the character of the speaker as well as report what was said. Feel free to use phrases like "Probably Dad said something like. . . ," or "As best I can recall he said. . . ," wherever it's appropriate to do so. It's important to present history, but it should be accurate, and that accuracy includes telling the reader when you are in doubt.

❋ **Use conversation creatively.** Don't use conversation just to convey information. Information is where exposition works fine. It sounds false to convey information for the reader in a conversation between people in the narrative: "Well Uncle Ed, here we are driving down Lake Shore Boulevard in Chicago on a fine October day in 1948." It is better to simply write, "It was a fine October day in 1948. As we drove down Lake Shore Boulevard, I said to my Uncle Ed. . . ."

✳ **Edit out "real" language?**   Paradoxically, conversation will not sound real if it accurately represents real speech; it will be so cluttered as to be unreadable. In real talk, people use words like *well* and *uh* to signal pauses and fill silences. If you report conversation like a transcript, you will drive off your readers. Suggest these words by using them only now and then. The same is true for phrases like "You know" and for profanity. Eavesdrop on a conversation and you'll see what I mean. Sit down in a coffeeshop with a notebook and pen and try to transcribe a conversation exactly. You'll hear something like this:

> Uh, why, hello there, uh, Sandy. How're you?
> Arthur! How're you? Gee. Well. What a surprise. Uh. You are—what are—where are you, I mean what are you up to these days? Huh? Uh?
> Well, I don't know. Ha. Uh. Well. I can't say much. Not much. Not much. I sure can't. Sure can't . . .

A little of this goes a long way and makes ordinary conversation sound silly and tedious. The conversation you write down on the page should be simplified, but still sound realistic. This isn't as hard as it might sound; common sense is a good guide. There's a difference between providing a record of the past like a court reporter and narrating it.

✳ **Editing selectively.**   Conversations can be reported directly and more or less totally, reported indirectly, or summarized. You might do all three in the same paragraph. For example:

> "I can't catch all these pigs myself, Esther," I said. Esther looked annoyed and told me she'd get home as soon as she could. When she got home I explained the problem: there were two or three holes in the fence and fifty-some pigs and they were going back out as fast as I could catch them and put them back, and the mothers were so upset I couldn't even get in the pen to fix the holes. "One of us will have to

keep her occupied while the other sneaks in and fixes the holes," I said. Esther told me to wait till she could change clothes, and left me standing there by the pen.

In the above example the sentences "I can't catch all these pigs myself, Esther" and "one of us will have to keep her occupied while the other sneaks in and fixes the holes" are of course directly reported. "Esther . . . told me she'd get home as soon as she could" and "Esther told me to wait till she could change clothes" are examples of indirect reporting; and "When she got home I explained the problem," etc., is an example of summarizing a conversation.

Please bear in mind that directly or indirectly reporting and summarizing conversations is something we do naturally in our talk all the time. If there is anything new here, it's the emphasis on presenting direct conversation, which we do less often—but still do—in our own talk. We might be telling our spouse about a conversation at the bank and we'll summarize the action and the conversation until we get to an important moment, and then we'll switch to direct quotation:

> Then—can you believe this?—he told me, "John, I can't loan you another cent."
>
> "If you can't loan me another cent," I told him, and I meant it too, "then you can just close my account right now."
>
> So he hemmed and hawed around. "Now wait a minute," he said.

All I'm suggesting is that you do a little more of what you already do when you tell a story. Conversation is too important for the historian to be left unused in the tool box.

☛ SUGGESTION:

In your journal, list each of your parents and grandparents (or your children, if you prefer), and under their name record at least three phrases they commonly used. These might be words they pronounced a distinct way, sayings they seem to be fond of repeating, or other phrases or whole sentences that they, for one reason or another, used abundantly. After I was grown and would come back home for a visit, my father and I would watch the evening news together. Eric Severeid, a famous commentator in that era, would come on for his five-minute reflection. My father would always lean over to me and say, "He's from North Dakota, you know." (We lived in North Dakota when I was a baby.) In addition, Dad had some unusual phrases. He said "allus" for always, though we finally teased him so much about it he finally used it only when he was around us to tease us back. He would say "Mom" for "Ma'am," which I guess was a hangover from the Cornish American town he grew up in in southern Wisconsin. He would say "on-huh," or something like that, when listening to a patient's description of his or her symptoms on the phone. Many times we would sit at the dinner table and smile at each other as we listened to half a conversation, something like this:

"On-huh."

"Oh-huh."

"Did you use the drops I gave you?"

"Oh, on-huh."

And so on. Everyone has their eccentricities, and they are clues to what kind of people they are. My father-in-law, a cattleman whose first language was German though he was born in Clay Center, Kansas, would take his sick animals to the "wetinarian." In your list, you'll have fun noting some of these defining characteristics of speech. If they spoke slowly or rapidly or hesitantly or uniquely in any other way, note that too. One man I knew for thirty years never, at least in my presence, finished a sentence. He would begin, "Ah, Charley, how nice. . . ," then switch to "What a beautiful morning it. . . ," and then change to an admiring comment about my shirt. It was an endearing characteristic—one I'll always remember about him. The words we speak and write are sometimes the most memorable things about us.

Suspense Isn't Just for Thrillers

If you were around in the 1940s there was one radio show you could not help knowing about. It began with an urbane gentleman saying something to the effect that tonight we were going to hear "a tale well calculated to keep you in suspense!" Everyone who was gathered around the radio hiked the chair a little bit closer and shivered with delight. And the tale that followed was always some ghoulish thing that sent us off to bed with our eyes wide open checking the nooks and crannies of the darkened bedroom.

It was great. We loved it. But *Suspense!* was to forever give us the wrong idea about the quality of suspense itself. We came to believe that it was limited to situations involving ax murderers creeping up on us from behind. It's not. We watch the lottery show to see if our numbers matter, and we are in suspense. We call to find out if we got a particular job, and we are in suspense. We get stopped by the police officer for speeding, who gives us a lecture as we wonder if the lecture is all we're going to get, and we are in suspense.

Life is necessarily suspenseful. We are always in doubt about what will happen next. And we use suspense in everyday conversations in very obvious ways:

Guess how much green beans cost at Food4Less?
You'll never believe what happened at the office today!
Who do you suppose is the new boss?

As a writer you should be aware of the quality of suspense and make use of it. It's a useful tool to keep your reader interested. Please don't think you are required to get some suspense into your writing. Probably a fair amount is already there simply because we tend to do that in narrative; it's almost a condition of narrative. Put suspense in when it seems natural or fun to do so. Be careful not to overuse it as too much will turn the reader off rather than on. You don't have to put an exploding cigar in every line; simple things will do. Here are a few easy ways:

1. If you are going to enumerate a series, tell the reader that upfront. Then he can tick them off with you, which helps keep him involved: "Dad took me to the woodshed just four times. The first was when I fought with my sister. The second was when . . ."

2. Give hints of what's to come: "Dad took me to the woodshed just four times, but the fourth time was a bit of a surprise for both of us."

3. Consider putting a title on your work that hints at an interesting story: "The Day I Started Life," "A Horse of a Different Color," or "The Vacation That Made Me Glad to Get Back to Work."

4. Raise a question in the reader's mind: "Digging potatoes can be fun." (It can? How so?) "My Uncle Jack had a fatal flaw." (What was it?)

5. Try starting in the middle of your story, which keeps the reader on the alert: "The kitchen was a mess." (How did it get that way? Who caused it?) "I do," I said. (Is this a wedding? Who's getting married?) "That was the last straw." (What was? Why?)

6. Do not trick or mislead your reader:

He walked into the room where she was sitting on the couch. He reached into his pocket. She looked up at him, her eyes big and round. He took out the chain. She stood up, terrified. Then he snapped the hook on the end of the chain around her collar and took the kittycat back outside.

Do this once, and your reader will never take you seriously again. Remember "The Boy Who Cried Wolf"?

Suspense is a tool that you can use to get and keep your reader's attention. You're competing with the noise of the TV in the next room, the hungry gurgle in the reader's tummy, the yawn, and the ringing of the phone, all of which are good reasons not to read what you've written. So you've got to give the reader a better reason to ignore those things and get on with what's really important: reading what you have to say.

If you have a suspenseful title or a suspenseful opening line (or both), chances are good the reader will stay with you. But remember that just as beauty is in the eye of the beholder, so also is suspense. The calculus of suspense isn't easy. It's a judgment that you as the writer must make about the nature of your readers.

Use Your Imagination

Another quality of the human mind helpful to the family history writer is the ability to imagine, to guess at what might be. Remember when you were little and you made shadows on the wall? All you had to do was extend a couple of opened fingers and an upright thumb and you and your friends would imagine that the shadow cast was that of a dog. Move the thumbs a little and it was a collie; a little differently and it was a spaniel. Writers depend on this ability to draw inferences, and as readers we do it all the time. We are so used to it, though, we may not be aware of it.

He answered the door. "Yes?" It was a young boy.
"I'm selling seeds. Want to buy some seeds?"

"Seeds? Well, no." The man looked down at the boy then. "Wait a minute. Whose boy are you? Do you live around here?"

"Yes, sir. I'm the Browns' son, Danny."

"Well Danny, what kind of seeds are you selling now?"

The writer doesn't have to explain what is in the man's mind. We can infer from what little we are told that the man has softened and that he is going to buy some seeds from this lad because he knows the family. Notice too that nothing needs to be said about a remarkable number of things that had to happen in this scene that we are not told about and automatically assume have happened. We are only told that "he answered the door." We are not told that the man grasped the doorknob and opened the door, for example, which we infer from the facts that are explicitly told.

Generally speaking, the more you can let your reader discover or imagine for themselves, the better. Telling the obvious can annoy readers because it interferes with the reality that you have created: it's as if you as a puppetmaster have your audience caught up in the scene between a couple of talking puppets, and then you stop and point out that you are manipulating bits of wood and cloth on a string. It destroys the illusion of reality you have worked so hard to build.

The Narrative Mix: Place, People, Action, and Narration

The more your story is a representation of life, the better. The highest compliment your reader can pay you is to unconsciously slip into the scene you are writing as an onlooker. We've probably had the experience of reading a horror story late at night with everyone else in bed that frightened us so that we double-check all the windows and doors before turning in. That's a tribute to the story's writer: the illusion created was so intense that you carry it over into your real life. That's just the sort of illusion you want to create, and you can do it.

You form the illusion by making it seem like what you are saying is happening is really happening. You create a setting, introduce your people, and have them move around and converse (think of yourself setting up a sort of doll house) by means of some of the techniques that I've described so far. One final point is to pay attention to the mix of all these things and make sure they are mixed and not simply inserted in chunks. This isn't difficult, but it does require that you pay attention to what you're writing and keep thinking: Is this the way it occurred?

Things happen all at once. While we're talking, we feel ourselves sitting on a cool chair, we hear the phone ring, and we see the neighbor's dog sniffing the ground out the window. We have to suggest that same pattern in our narrative.

> "Why do I have to clean my room now, Mom?" I asked. The phone rang. "Hello," I said.
>
> "Because I said so," Mom said. She looked at me in mock anger and shook her finger, but I knew she meant it.
>
> "Alice! How are you?" I said into the phone, sliding into the leather chair. The leather felt cool against my bare legs. "Can you go to the dance?" I glanced at Mom, smiled, and stuck out my tongue, then mouthed the words All right. Then I turned to the window and put my feet up on the sill, looking out at the Haley's dog Blackie sniffing at a hole in the ground, and went on talking to Alice.

This sort of careful and constant mixing gives the reader the impression of many stimuli and leads the reader to trust you to present reality. You don't have to do it all the time—you couldn't and make sense—but you have to do it enough so that the illusion of reality is established and maintained.

☞ SUGGESTION:

Write a scene a page or two long from your own life, perhaps from something as recent as yesterday. Any scene in which you are talking to someone else will do. Present the conversation, but also be careful to make the reader aware of where you are and what might be happening besides the conversation.

The Slice of Life Versus a Beginning, Middle, and End

In literature, a story is supposed to have a beginning, a middle, and an end. Sometimes people assume that family history does too. Understandably, they want to tell or write stories that involve the reader, and so they tend to write only about the high points of their life, the big moments, and since for most of us there aren't many big moments (as we see it), would-be historians often conclude that they have nothing to write about—no stories, just sketches of this and that which don't lead anywhere. What have you done all your days but get up and go to work and come home and eat supper and sit around for an hour or two and get up the next morning and do the same thing all over again?

We all know this is a very superficial view, but it does have enough truth to it to sometimes make us think we have nothing to say. Or maybe you can get past the idea that your life is no more and no less humdrum than everybody else's but—you tell yourself in this grim mood you're in—you have no imagination! If you had any imagination, you reason, you could think of the hilarious, the dramatic, the exceptional moments of your life. But no, you tell yourself, you don't have any. So there you are, stuck. Or maybe you're driving downtown and in your stoplight reveries you think of an episode that might be interesting to write about, but when you get home you think that no one would be interested.

As with any other writing problem, there are specific things you can do to change this perspective. Mostly it just requires a little attitude adjustment. Don't try to be "imaginative." Don't even try to be interesting. Instead, just try to be honest. And instead of trying to think of some Big Moment, think of your life as a loaf of bread. Cut off a slice and describe it. Just describe what you see in your mind's eye: the plain, unvarnished truth as you see it.

Don't spend more than a few minutes thinking about where to slice that loaf. Just start writing. For example, maybe a memory pops into your head of the day you were in fourth grade and during recess Tommy Pfitzmeier threw an apple at you, missed, and broke a window in the school building. As you tell the story, think of yourself as an artist, painting the scene with words:

> Tommy Pfitzmeier yelled something. I yelled something back. He grinned and revealed that he held in his hand one of the pulpy old apples the cafeteria was doling out. He must have been about fifty feet from me. He raised the apple as if to throw it.
>
> "I dare you," I yelled. I never thought the dummy would do it.
>
> He leaned back like a baseball pitcher and let fly. I ducked, but the window to Mrs. Archer's room couldn't move, and the apple crashed right through it.

The other kids playing around us stopped. All eyes went to the broken window. Mrs. Archer magically appeared. All eyes, hers included, looked at Tommy and then at me.

Mrs. Archer waggled her finger. At Tommy? At me? "Both of you," she said. "Come inside. Right now."

I thought, Why me? and followed Tommy into the school-house.

And so on. Notice that I did not try to tell *about* that time, and I didn't try to be a reporter objectively describing the scene for his readers. All I tried to do was draw what I saw in my thoughts. The only responsibility you have when you narrate from your own point of view, as I have done here, is to draw what you see. That's the beauty of it. It's really very simple. All you do is cut off a slice of your life and make us see it.

Contrast this with the usual idea of story as a narrative with a climax or a literary form with a "meaning." *Moby Dick* is such a story. So is *The Scarlet Letter*. In the twentieth century in both literature and history, the idea of meaning is less pronounced. More and more, there is a tendency for writers of fiction and history to suggest that their job is essentially to present experience and not so much interpret it or arrange it to fit someone's idea of meaning. It might even seem that the two forms of fiction and history are merging.

A better model than the Big Moment story is, as I have suggested, that of the genre painters who painted everyday life. For example, George Caleb Bingham, an unpretentious nineteenth-century Missouri painter, is an excellent model for what we might call genre history. As you write your family history, you might think of yourself as a genre writer, portraying the everyday life of yourself and your family. Just as Bingham did not worry about telling a story, all you need to do is honestly and realistically portray what you see in your mind's eye. The scene you write, like the one in Fig. 2–1, doesn't have to have a beginning, a middle, and an end. It just is.

Think of a scene from your life as a child at home with your parents or as a young adult making your way in the world or as a parent or grandparent. You might be a child absorbed in playing with a yo-yo; a young woman carefully working at her typewriter on the first day of a new job in Omaha far from the farm where she grew up; a parent fixing dinner before the world became microwavable; or a grandparent reading a story in a book to a grandchild.

Your scene should not be static like a painting. But you need not tell a snappy and crackling tale that ends with a shiver or guffaw. It's

FIG. 2–1   *A scene as history: George Caleb Bingham's* Canvassing for a Vote

enough to carefully and realistically portray that moment in time. Set the scene, lavish it with detail, be true to your memory, and you will have written history.

Enjoy What You're Writing

Sometimes in conversation it seems we are reluctant to take up the time of the listener, and so we summarize and come quickly to the point: "I ran into Esther at the grocery and we talked and talked and she invited us for dinner Saturday night." "That's nice," your inattentive spouse says behind the newspaper. You don't go into any detail about what you "talked and talked" about, what fun it was, how Esther reminded you of your Aunt Pearl with her quick wit and laughing ways, how you enjoyed her, and how she enjoyed your enjoyment, how glad you were to have run into her, and how all your shopping was done and now you had this time to chatter away with an old friend.

Events that might seem to be boring can be extremely interesting when detailed. One of the real pleasures of writing is to slow down and examine a "boring" moment closely. Take another look at Sandra Gregersen's account of her few moments with her father in the dairy barn back on p. 27. What might have been in summary rather boring ("After school I'd go to the barn and help Dad for awhile") becomes in detail a fascinating and vivid account of the author's life and her relationship with her father.

Focus your magnifying lens on what's important to you and bring it forth in all its rich detail. Do not be in a hurry to get it over with. If you're in a hurry, chances are you're bored. And if you are in a hurry to write it, you can be sure the reader will be in a much bigger hurry to read it.

How to Get the Best Out of Yourself

Good writing doesn't come to the person who sits and waits for "inspiration." Good writing comes as a result of perspiration. I've tried sitting and waiting for inspiration. Whole days went by, and nothing much happened. Every writer I have ever known has concluded the same thing. Yet there are times that are unproductive when writing as with anything else. You sit down at your appointed times and whittle away but nothing much comes of it. You seem to just be filling the page. You're going through the motions. That is when you should stop writing and do something else for a while—a few minutes, hours, days, or even a week or two. Go away from where you write—the screen, the desk, the tablet. Go for a walk in the woods, go out for the evening, do something very different from what you've been doing. Socialize, relax, don't think about it.

Chances are when you come back some of the problems that were interfering will have disappeared or solved themselves. They will not seem to be the problems that they were. I have seen this happen again and again in my own writing life and in the life of students and other writers I know. You will find what works best for you. The truth is that everyone develops a personal way of working.

Care About What You're Writing

If writing isn't going well, it may be you're writing about something that you feel ought to be a part of your biography or history of your grandparents' lives together but just isn't interesting or meaningful to you. It's not your angle, cup of tea, or passion. So you plod and feel dutiful. But maybe it would be better to get on with writing something you genuinely care about. To write with heart, feeling, and a sense of the urgency and importance of what you are trying to communicate to the reader—to write as if you had her by the shoulders and were looking directly into her eyes as you spoke to her—is what you want. It's largely a matter of learning to write about those things that you care about.

This seems simple enough, and it is. But it's easy to confuse what you think ought to be important with what is. What we think and what we feel are sometimes two different things. I might think it's very important to write about my grandmother, but in fact I didn't know her very well and she wasn't very important in my life. On the other hand, an old man to whom I was not related, my employer through junior and senior high school, was very important to me. In those years of adolescent rebellion, I valued his esteem almost more than I did my father's, and I know that when I write about that man I care a lot about what I'm saying. Read the following family story and see if you don't sense a writer who cares deeply about what she's telling you.

Jim and Me
by Syble Bibb

The summer of 1947 Jimmy was fourteen and I was twelve. Jimmy and I didn't get along. Jimmy liked to argue, tease, and aggravate. Mama would say, "You two act like you hate each other."

"I do. I hate him!" I cried.

"Un-uh," Jimmy smiled. "I love her and I love to hear her holler."

Jimmy was a loner. He never played with Paul or me. He would be off by himself playing until he got tired of being alone. He would hunt Paul and me up, then start a fight by tearing up the things we were playing with. Mama said that for years she thought her name had been changed to "Mama Make," as that was the way all of us kids greeted her. Mostly it was "Mama make Jimmy quit."

There was seven of us kids and Mama and Daddy in our family. Usually there were two or three other people living with us. Meal time was always hectic. Long benches sat on each side of the dining table. The table was long enough that fourteen people could easily be comfortable while eating. Jimmy sat on a bench on one side and my place was directly opposite him. If Jimmy saw me look up from my plate he would hunch his shoulders forward until his chest caved in, then he would work the sides of his mouth until the leaders in his neck stood up in tight, ugly ridges.

"Mama, make Jimmy quit making faces," I cried.

Mama looked at Jimmy. He had this angelic look and innocently said, "Mama, I'm not making faces." As soon as Mama looked away the face contortions started again.

Mama made cornbread in cast-iron skillets and turned the bread out onto plates, bottom side up. Before she had cut it into wedges, Jimmy would look at me, then break off a piece. Before the crust broke, he would lift up and pull and take the crust off of about half of the corn bread. I hate corn bread without any crust.

When a girlfriend came to visit there was Jimmy. "Give me a kiss, Joanne," Jimmy would say and we would run, yelling to Mama, "Make Jimmy leave us alone."

"If you will just take him down and kiss the living fool out of him, he will leave you alone," Mama said. "He's just doing it to aggravate you."

We tried and it worked for a little while. When Jimmy came into the kitchen again, Joanne and I tackled him. We kissed him all over his face and neck and wouldn't let him up off the kitchen floor. He laughed and begged us to let him up. We did and the rest of that day he left us alone.

Jimmy loved to sing and whistle. Everyone knew where he was at any given moment. All we had to do was listen. Coming through the fields Jimmy was either singing, whistling, or playing his harmonica. He wanted to be able to speak Spanish but had no one to teach him. We could hear him as he brought the cows from the pasture.

"Ah yah yah Rancho Grande. Ah yah yah monto seeee yah," he would sing.

"Here comes old Jim singing his Mexican song," we would say.

One Saturday in late June I was standing at the dining table, washing dishes and daydreaming. We washed dishes in a blue granite dish pan, then took the water to the edge of the yard to empty it. Jimmy walked through the kitchen and as he passed me he said, "You are so ugly, you stink," and went out the back door.

If I could just get back at him. He always had me mad, crying, or yelling. I stood with my hands in the dish water trying to think of some way to get even. Through the kitchen window I saw him going toward the toilet.

"Ne—ta. Waa haa haa ne—ta. Ask thy soul if we should part," I heard him sing.

Suddenly I knew what I would do. I snickered to myself and ran to look out the kitchen window. I wanted to know when he started from the toilet as timing was essential. Two seconds either too fast or too slow and the whole scheme would be ruined.

Jim strolled from the toilet, stopped to pet his brindle bulldog, then slowly sauntered toward the back door, whistling. As soon as he reached the bottom step I snatched up the dish pan, hurried to the back door, kicked the screen door open and flung the cold, greasy dish water slap smack in Jimmy's face. Little pieces of food hung to the front of his shirt. Water dribbled from his face. His hair lay plastered to his head. The dish rag landed on his shoulder. He looked so surprised.

I knew I was in for it. He would beat the living daylights out of me. I ran down the steps. "Oh, Jim! I'm sorry. I didn't know you were there." I helped him wipe off and he sort of grinned.

For years every time I thought about that I remembered how funny he looked and how he didn't get mad. Jimmy later went into the Marine Corps, and married a Mexican girl. She taught him Spanish. They have three sons.

For over twenty years he was a policeman for the Albuquerque, New Mexico, police force. He was an undercover detective for the last few years. When he was forty-eight he had a motorcycle accident that damaged his brain stem. His motor mechanism and his short-term memory were damaged. He is now being cared for in a nursing home. All women other than his wife, he calls Syble.

The selection of scenes about her brother, the magnificent characterization of her brother that makes him seem in just a few lines so real to us, and putting her name as the very last word of the story are all done with great talent. Did the author have these skills and simply put them to use, or did she have heart and did the heart evoke the skills? Probably both.

☞ SUGGESTION:

Try to make a list of ten of the most important things in your life. I mean anything—your feelings about your children or your job, for example, as a social worker, helping those who can't seem to help themselves. Be very specific, and be honest. Some things in your life that you've given a lot of time to might seem like they ought to be of great interest to you. But perhaps they really and finally were not. Don't just list items. Make a complete sentence, a statement.

A Refreshing Digression

Digression is a close relative to writing on what you care deeply about. We've all read stories with sections that didn't quite fit in with the rest of what was being said; the author obviously wanted to digress in some detail. Often, readers welcome such digressions even if the section seems out of place.

If you tend to digress now and then, go ahead and do it. It's probably something that you care about or you wouldn't have gotten carried away. However, if you find yourself doing this often, particularly if you find yourself digressing from one digression to another and forgetting where you started out, then it's probably time to get yourself back on track. I use "probably" here because I have read memoirs that were basically one digression after another and yet they were still enjoyable reading. There is no hard and fast rule here. If you're a digressing person, maybe it's best to digress away and hope the reader will accept that. It will certainly be much more preferable than not writing anything at all. I bring up the subject here to encourage those who are fearful of seeming disorganized to go ahead and enjoy it. Probably the reader will appreciate the digression as much as you.

Your Sense of Humor

You have a sense of humor, so allow it to enter into your writing. I don't mean sticking in your favorite jokes. Humor is a kind of knowledge, a way of looking at the world. It's something you've been refining all your life. It should be a part of your writing, which above all should reflect your personality. What you find funny is one way of measuring what you've learned in life. Yet humor is often looked upon by "serious" people as something like the opposite of knowledge and wisdom. It's light stuff, entertainment. But there isn't or shouldn't be a contradiction between being informative and being entertaining.

Take a moment to consider what you find funny. Humor has as many forms as the faces that express it. We laugh, we smile, we chuckle, we chortle, we giggle, we guffaw. We roar with laughter, we laugh until we cry, grin good naturedly, or smile wryly.

How can you put humor in the history of your life? You probably shouldn't try. I would simply encourage you not to suppress it when it tries to enter into your writing. In other words, don't take yourself too seriously. You probably have more humor in you than you think, even if you aren't the sort of person who pulls a friend aside to tell the latest joke. Consider the following short memoir by Patrick Hudson. Notice how the humor is really built in to the way Patrick looks at the world. From another point of view, this story could be sad, but when Patrick tells us his version he is also telling us about how he has learned to look at life.

Winter Memories
by Patrick Hudson

It's hard to imagine that in 1930 most people in Michigan lived in uninsulated houses. We did. Storm windows were a luxury. We didn't miss them because we hadn't seen them. Frost an eighth of an inch thick covered our windows and made them into slate boards where I learned to write my name. Our furnace had just one register. It was in the dining room, which was the center of the house.

I still slept in a crib although I was seven years old. It was in the room that had been the attic until it was pressed into use as a bedroom. Mom had a stoneware jug that held about a half gallon of hot water. She used that to warm my bed. I put on my Doctor Denton sleepers downstairs and she tucked me in bed. I was tucked in so well that someone (my sister) had to help me get up in the morning.

The house had wooden shingles and I could lay in bed in the morning and see daylight through the roof. These shingles would swell up when it started to rain so they didn't leak. Snow melted off and formed big icicles all around the house.

We were used to cold and wore heavy clothes. Cars did-
n't have heaters but we had a sedan and compared to a
Model T it was stuffy to my folks.

We had an ice storm that winter that was beautiful.
Everything was coated with ice except our roof. The ice
melted, ran down the porch roof, filled up the eavestrough,
dripped down on the front steps, and froze.

Our next-door neighbor, Ray Wise, was a large, friendly
man. He was my dad's best friend. He came over to call that
morning.

Our front screen door opened outward right at the top
of the steps. This made it difficult to open the door if you
came up the steps too far. Ray was too far up and the bottom of the screen door was stuck in the ice. He was strong
and determined. He pulled hard, the door swung open, and
since he was standing on ice he found himself sliding all the
way to the street on his stomach.

Dad helped Ray up the steps and brushed him off. Ray
wasn't hurt but he was upset. He was irate. He kept saying,
"You should have salt or ashes on those steps. Suppose your
parents had fallen like that!"

My sister and I wanted to laugh but my aunt kept looking at us with her lips pursed and shaking her head slightly.
My dad and mother didn't dare look at each other.

Dad decided to empty his ashtray. Really he just wanted
to get out of the house so he could laugh. His ashtray was a
brass bowl, made in India, about six inches in diameter. It
must have weighed almost a pound.

In his haste to get out of the house he forgot that the
back steps would also be covered with ice. He stepped on
the top step, slipped, threw up his arms to catch himself,
lost hold of the brass bowl and ran down the steps across
the drive and stopped at the grape arbor.

He had this timed exactly because he got there at the
same time that the bowl did. It sounded like a Chinese gong
when it him on the head. He was on his hands and knees,
the long hair that he covered his bald spot with hanging
over his eyes.

Mom hurried to the rescue, slipped, stumbled, and fell
on him. My sister caught my aunt who was about to follow
and probably saved Dad from being flattened again.

With everyone back inside we started laughing. Ray told Dad that he looked like an English sheep dog on his knees with his hair over his eyes. Dad was still laughing at the sight of Ray sliding down the front walk, and I was laughing because everyone else was laughing.

☞ SUGGESTION:

List as many situations in your or your family's life that you find funny as you can. (Define "funny" in your own way or ways.)

The Role of Revision

It is often said the real excitement in writing comes in revision, and this is true in some kinds of writing, particularly very intense writing like poetry. Professional writers like to brag sometimes about how hard they work and how much revision they do. The history of literature is filled with stories about writers who revised and revised. Hemingway is said to have rewritten the ending of *A Farewell to Arms* thirty-seven times. Tolstoy rewrote his very long novel *War and Peace* seven times.

But I think the value of revision is oversold, and in no area of writing is this truer than in family history. In personal narrative, especially, I am suspicious of revision. I fear that more might be lost in revision than gained. That is, it's possible to lose the authenticity that is so very, very important in personal narrative. After all, if the reader can't believe the language of such a narrative, what's it worth?

Of course the decision of whether or not to revise can only be your own. If you are a reviser, go to it with a gentle hand. Be careful if you find yourself writing something and then setting it aside because you want someday to revise it. That may simply mean that you're trying to avoid its being read and, you may fear, being judged.

Nowhere do I mean to suggest that the writing of family history can be slapdash because it can't compare with "real" history or literature. But family history should have a homemade look to it and should have the flavor of the people it's about. For minor revisions, I suggest that you rewrite and recast sentences as you go along, which is easy if you write on a word processor or a computer. Beyond that, it's up to you. Better to write more than rework endlessly. Good family narratives are often more the product of a relaxed and comfortable writer than they are of someone slaving over a hot typewriter.

Most emphatically, family history is not a poor second or third cousin to what "real writers" do. I can't think of anything more important than to write my family's history and the story of my life for my children. These are the people I know and love. How much more meaningful to write for them than for strangers! Instead of asking yourself if what you have written is "good" in some comparative, objective sense, ask instead, Does this writing sound like me? Is this my voice, my way of looking at the world, and my way of expressing it? Does it reflect my experience? Is it what my family needs from me?

To this end, the single best thing you can do in deciding whether and how much to revise is to read your work out loud to hear if that's really you writing. You might even tape it and listen to it. If it's you, then it's right and your children will thank you for being yourself.

The Forms of
Family History

I met a man who told me the only family history he would ever write would be autobiography. "That's fine," I said. "Where do you want to begin?"

"Why, with the day I was born."

"You don't *have* to begin with that, you know," I said, and went on to explain how the day we were born wasn't necessarily all that significant compared to moments from our life that are charged with meaning. But before I got very far with my little sermon, this man, a retired minister, interrupted.

"I wouldn't even think of reading an autobiography that didn't begin with the first day of one's life."

He was a serious, solemn man, sitting on the couch frowning at me, and he added that he was thinking about including a good many of his sermons in his autobiography. I swallowed and did my best to smile. "That sounds just fine," I said. In teaching adults over the years I've learned to let them do it their way, to step back and give them plenty of room.

I never saw this gentleman's autobiography. I never met him again. But I have a hunch he never wrote one. Starting with the first day of his life and working straight ahead was logical and very tidy. But such a strategy seldom gets beyond planning because not much happened on the first day of anybody's life or the first few years of life that we remember anything about or, far more important, have strong feelings about.

It often works better to adopt a casual approach and write up histories in small pieces, scenes from our own life and our family's life, and in no particular order. Most of the people I work with through *LifeStory* will write several pieces about a certain area of their life—their time in school, for example—and then move to another area and write several pieces about that period or topic, and so on. When publication time comes, of course, then these sections can be arranged in chronological (or any other) order.

In the following chapters I discuss and present examples of some of the ways I know of recording family history in manageable pieces. Most of them have been suggested by examples sent to me in my capacity as the editor of *LifeStory*. These "forms," as I am calling them, are not at all rigid and are meant only to be suggestions of possible directions you might want to explore. You will adapt and reinvent as you write, so that your family history bears your own imprint and style. Truly, the medium is the message. And this is appropriate particularly if you are writing a family history that is to a considerable degree the story of your life.

The first three forms—journal, interviews, and photo-caption writing—are the most important, I believe, but the rest are listed in ascending order of difficulty, ending with a chapter on writing a family newsletter and another on writing autobiographical fiction.

The Narrative Journal

✳ **Why keep a journal?**　I can think of five good reasons to keep a journal. First, unless the family historian writes things down, he has nothing but a head full of research. A journal is in this regard a sort of second head, a file cabinet of your thoughts. You may or may not intend for your journal to be anything other than a record of your thoughts and research. But the fact is that a large part of the world's history, public and private, comes directly from journals that were written by people who never intended them to be seen by anybody but themselves. Indeed, much of what we know about life in seventeenth-century London comes from Samuel Pepys' diary.

Second, a journal conditions you as a writer just as jogging or weightlifting conditions you physically. It also makes you into a writer, not just a wannabe writer. This may seem a trivial goal, though I'm convinced it quickly leads to a change of attitude toward what you are doing. Like a pro, it gets you writing every day. *Daily* is the key word. There is no real distinction between the terms *journal* and *diary*, but both words have their origin in the Latin word *diurnalis*, which means "diurnal" or "daily." It works best to write every day, preferably at the same time. Set it up so that you find yourself saying, "It's seven in the morning, time to write in my journal," or, "It's bedtime, time to write in my journal." Writing becomes not something you do when the muse is around and you're in the mood, but a part of your everyday life. You may not be thinking of yourself as a writer, only as someone who wants to write a family history; but it will help if, for now at least, you think of yourself as a professional.

A third reason for you to keep a journal is for its direct usefulness in writing family history. Journaling inevitably encourages family historians not only to write their own and their family's past, but to be "historians of the present," chroniclers of ongoing family life. By your journal's everpresence in your everyday life, you are inevitably going to sit down and find yourself thinking not only of the distant past, but also of the present: a fight with your spouse over money, a discussion with a co-worker about how to approach a new project, or some priceless thing one of your children or grandchildren said or did. Unavoidably and gloriously, a journal becomes a family archive and album. If you index your journal as you go along that will make it that much more useful.

Fourth, journaling stimulates your memory. Since you're writing every day, you can draw on your memories almost as they occur. Actually, it is life that stimulates memory. The journal simply permits you to get it on the record. You are standing in the checkout line at the grocery and the woman in front of you has red hair and green eyes or a lilt in her voice like your Aunt Marie used to have, and so you remember and slip into a reverie of the summer you spent with her and Uncle Bill at their beach house long, long ago. When a few hours later you sit down to write in your journal that reminiscence is still fresh in your mind and you can write it down. Instead of sitting down to write about that time "cold" and staring at a blank screen or page because at that particular moment memory doesn't serve, you can write the memories in your journals as they come to you. I don't agree, by the way, with the old saw that "if a thing's worth remembering, you won't forget it." That may be true of some things, but it seems to me that just as often the opposite is true: We tend to forget or repress those things that really are important.

Fifth, writing every day in a journal allows you to practice and experiment. It allows you to try and fail and try again another day. Imagine a pianist who never practiced. A journal can be a kind of first draft for any writing you do. You get used to confronting the real problems that writers face all the time: how to give the impression of a crowd, how to show two old friends excitedly talking at once, how to make the reader feel and see a beautiful spring day. If you had to write these or other challenging moments "for the record," you might find the task so daunting that you would not do it at all. A journal gets you to do it, and if you like what you do, you can copy it out and publish it. If you don't, you can try again another day.

Since a journal is written a page at a time, it gets you used to thinking of your writing project as merely the next day's entry. Often contemplation of an entire project is mind boggling; it is too much, too monumental a task. But a journal gets you into the habit of downsizing, of cutting those impossibly big jobs into manageable scenes.

✳ The beneficial side effects of journaling.　After you have kept a journal for a few months, you will probably find that the act of sitting down and writing gives you a high something like the same way jogging does for the habitual runner. I do not know that the body chemistry of journalers has been studied like that of joggers, but I wouldn't be surprised to find that there are similarities. It may be compulsive, but it's compulsiveness in a good cause. Fulfilling your compulsion every day is—well, fulfilling. You may find it satisfying— most journalers do—to see the pages stack up. It's worth pointing out that if you write a page a day with an average length of about three hundred words, in only six months you will have written a book.

You will find also that writing in a journal is cathartic in the same sense that talking anything out with a friend, loved one, or even a stranger is. Many psychotherapists, in fact, ask their patients to keep a journal as an additional tool in the healing process.

✳ How I keep my journal.　I have kept a journal for more than thirty years. That's not especially long as journals go, and only in the last ten years or so have I required myself to write daily. Aside from the mechanical requirements of writing at a certain time every day for a certain length, I am very undemanding. I do require myself to write every morning as soon as I get up. I write fifty-four lines, the number of lines on a page of my word processor program. I have done this for so long and am so rigid about this that if I do miss because of sickness or absence, I am out of sorts. This is just the way I want it. When I finish my journal, usually before breakfast, I feel like I have already done a good day's work. If nothing else happens that day, if I were to spend the entire day watching soap operas and reruns on TV, I have accomplished something: I wrote in my journal. I have written five hundred words.

Whether they are good words or not isn't terribly material. Of

course I feel great if I've written some challenging scene to my satisfaction. But I don't feel bad if I've only filled in the page, because I
feel that filling in the page is important. I do not revise what I've
written in the journal. I tried that for a week many years ago. In that
terrible week I thought I'd try warming up each day by revising the
previous day's work. After a week of rewriting Sunday's entry, I quit
revising. Getting any project to work is always a matter of compro-
mising competing goals. I realized that if I was going to go for highly
polished prose in my journal, I wasn't going to be able to keep a journal. I decided a journal was more important, and so I opted for mini-
mal revision.

I do a little "spot revising" in the form of recasting a sentence
now and then before I write it down, or even—now that I use a computer and changes are so much easier—I might change a sentence
slightly once I've written it. But I am very tolerant: what comes out
the first time is usually what I put down. I try to make the act of writing spontaneous, pleasant, and easy. I may pull something out of the
journal and rewrite it for publication, for use in a class, or for some
other purpose, but I do not revise journal entries.

I look forward to writing every morning in the journal. It is one
of the happiest times of the day. I commune with myself. Sometimes
I feel it is like prayer. Nor do I plan very much in advance. In order
to avoid sitting and trying to think of what to write about, however,
I write myself notes. I work at home, and all over the house I keep
pads of paper and a ball point pen. Kitchen or bathroom, basement
tool room or bedroom, I have in each a pad of paper and a pen.
Whenever I'm away from my house I have a pen and paper in my
pocket. In my car I have a setup on the dashboard. It's a little eccen-
tric, but I figure I'm a writer, so why not? As I go about my day's
work, at home or away, I have random thoughts. When something
interesting occurs to me, something I might like to explore further in
writing, I jot it down. It might be a memory from my past: "Uncle
Pete teaching Gary and me to play poker," or, "The shining look on
June's face when the nurse handed Rip to her." It might be some com-
plaint: "People who don't use the turn signals on their thirty-thou-
sand-dollar cars." Or a question, "What am I going to do when my
kids are all grown and gone?"

At the end of the day I take all these notes from my pocket and
put them by the keyboard of my word processor. The next day I get
up and there they are, ready and waiting. I pick them up one by one
and write about them. Of course, some days I don't get through all
the notes. Though sometimes I go beyond my one-page require-

ment, usually I don't, and so the notes may stack up. That's okay. The only problem is when I can't read my handwriting and can't remember what I wrote down.

On any given day I may write about one single thing or half a dozen different things. I might write two lines about a cat that had kittens, a whole paragraph about a phone conversation with my mother, and then a short scene showing my son and me working on his car the night before.

Yes, there are bad days. Most of those that start out badly do not end up that way. I'm usually able to kid myself out of my bad mood that sometimes comes with a gray, cold morning. Sometimes I write something like the following:

> One nice thing about computers is that now when I sit and stare at the screen I can watch the cursor pulse. It's like watching my own pulse, my own heart beat, my own and only life tick away as I stare myself in and out of a trance.

Then I go to work. I can only say of all these techniques that they work for me. Something else might work better for you.

❋ Understanding narrative journals. I have called the type of journal I use a *narrative* journal, and that's an important distinction. When possible, I do try to make my entries narratives. This is not a demand I make on myself so much as a tactic for getting the best writing done.

Think of each day as one narrative segment after another. You get up in the morning, wash and dress, eat, go to work, and so on all through the day until you come home and go to bed that night. Even in sleep there are narratives in dreams, and I often write them too.

Without getting too philosophical here, I want to point out that ideas about life come from the stories of life and not the other way around. And so I trust concrete knowledge—narratives—more than I do abstracted knowledge. This reflects the point I made earlier in the book that history is a narrative, and the more narrative the better.

Narrative is also easier and more natural to write. For example, suppose you start your journal and you write at the top of the page the date "June 10" and the year and you remember that June 10 was about the time you took your first real job, that summer after high school in 1950 when you were going with Ed Gibbons and both of you worked at Pearl's Restaurant. You write,

I walked in all dressed up and asked for a job waiting tables. Ed was in the back washing dishes and he saw me and winked, because it was Ed who had suggested I apply. The boss didn't know we even knew each other, Ed and I, much less that we were going together.

See how effortlessly this becomes a story? And if it seems just like conversation, so much the better; you're on the right track. A journal is a sort of conversation with yourself, or any friendly, interested listener you might care to imagine. The narrative should flow easily and naturally, just as you might tell a story.

Although my journal has its share of summaries, I do not try to summarize my day. I know people who write things like, "Up at eight, bacon and eggs over easy for breakfast, then off to work on the 7:30 train." I don't write this way. It may serve some purpose for the writer, but barring courtroom testimony requirements it probably doesn't serve much purpose. I know many journalers, though, myself included, who do enter a certain amount of important data. One farmer I know uses her journal to record births among her and her husband's cattle. But normally not even you are going to be interested in reading what you had for breakfast in the future. Instead, tell a story, set the scene, and write,

"Bacon and eggs again?" Rip said at breakfast. "I hate bacon and eggs."

"What do you mean?" June said. "You love bacon and eggs!" She shoveled a couple of sunny-side up eggs onto his plate.

He took his fork and started eating but did not stop complaining. "Mom, I don't like them every morning of the world."

"We haven't had bacon and eggs every morning," June said.

"Not since yesterday morning," I said.

She looked at me. "Did we have bacon and eggs yesterday?"

"You don't even remember!" Rip said, and we all laughed.

"I like bacon and eggs," I said. "I could eat them every morning of the world. But where's my toast?"

"Can't you make your own?" June said. "Sor-ry!"

This will be fun to read—at least in my own family—years from now because it shows us in action and reveals character. Summary is only useful to get to scene. One scene like this might be a whole day's entry, but my feeling is that a scene like this reveals far more, and is far more interesting to read, than a whole page of notations about what was eaten and weather reports. Humans cannot live by data alone.

I try to write honestly and freely without regard for someone looking over my shoulder. I never show my journal to anyone. It is entirely and strictly personal and my family respects that. The journal is as private and intimate as my own mind. Indeed, sometimes it is my mind, almost a transcript of my thoughts. I think it's very important to write that way, and some others I know do also, but some do not. I do write down negative thoughts about myself and others, even people I love. I may change my mind the next day, but I have no regrets. If the journal helps me rid myself of negative thoughts, so much the better. I feel that I am responsible for my acts but I am not responsible for my thoughts.

❋ What do you do with your journal?   "If I keep a journal as you recommend," I am sometimes asked, "what will happen to it when I die?" Usually questions come from people who are concerned about the effect of their candid and possibly negative thoughts or their intimate life on loved ones. If you have written for yourself as I recommend, opening up your whole mind without reservation or censorship, there may well be a great deal in your journal that will be, you think, offensive to your family.

We have negative thoughts about all those we love, and I think we have to assume that those we love will be understanding enough to accept that. Why not grant them this level of understanding?

But if this isn't satisfactory, you can also purge your journal regularly, though I would encourage you to be careful: you may want that later. It's also possible to write a letter and place it in your will to some third party whom you have designated to be a literary executor of your estate to go over your journals and other literary productions with a view toward editing out negative material.

Try a journal for at least a month, and preferably longer. Even if you feel you are in the twilight of your life, it is not too late to use a journal as an easy, natural, and effective way to produce a thorough family history. A few lines a day of family history quickly add up. And I don't know anyone who has kept a journal for a year or more who doesn't love it or wonder how they got along without it before. For me, it's often the happiest time of day. All I have to do is sit and sip my coffee and write. What could one want beyond that? It's one of the purest pleasures I know.

☞ SUGGESTION:

In your journal, tell the story of an idea you have recently had. Maybe lately as you've gone about your work you've developed and/or refined an idea you've had about how to fix mashed potatoes, what Congress ought to do about the welfare system, or what your youngest child likes to watch on TV. Ideas come from our experience. Write the experience that led to the idea you choose.

Interviews

❋ **Recording your interviews.**   It may seem out of place in a book on writing family history to recommend that you tape record any interview you conduct. But a tape recorder is, among other things, a valuable tool for writers. It allows historians to get everything down in an interview but leaves them free to be a real participant—not just a sort of recording secretary—in the conversation. This is important, because getting a good interview may depend on your ability to seem natural and relaxed and genuinely interactive with the person or persons you're interviewing.

But taping is more than a tool or means to an end. The tapes will be a valuable addition to any history you write. So use them to help your memory when you write history but also keep them in your files as part of that history. (Everything I'm saying here about audiotaping applies equally to videotaping. But since video camcorders are still somewhat exotic for most of us, I am limiting my remarks to audiotaping.)

Start by interviewing the older members of your family just as soon as you possibly can. Even if they may be busily at work writing their history, try to get them to reminiscence with you on tape. The sound of a person's voice tells things the written word cannot. Imagine owning a tape of your great-grandparents discussing their arrival in this country a hundred years ago. Most of us have relatives in their eighties or older, still quite alert and in good voice. Imagine what it will be like a hundred years from now for your great-grandchildren to listen to your mother's voice on tape, talking about her life as a young girl 150 years earlier! The technology is there, cheap and easy to use. It would be a shame not to get some of these "living libraries" on tape.

There is a double victory here most of the time. Not only does history win, but sometimes the person being interviewed is enabled to review life with many of the same effects that a writer of an autobiography or memoir would experience. I have had the privilege of conducting taped and untaped sessions of more or less systematic reminiscence on a number of occasions in nursing homes, and the effect is usually spectacular. Depressed, bored people come to life as they laugh and talk about their childhood and youth, remembering the games they played or the friends they had. Interviewing was a deeply moving experience for me as well.

It's not necessary or even desirable to transcribe taped interviews. For some reason, it's hard to get people to accept this, particularly older people. Often in workshops some diligent and well-meaning individual will ask if there is any way to speed up the transcribing process. My only answer is to stop doing it. Tapes keep. It's true that writing has been around for a few thousand years and taping only for a couple of generations, but it's clearly here to stay. If tapes get old and brittle, make a new one. What's the difference between giving your grandchild a book of your family history and giving her a tape she can pop into the car stereo and listen to as she drives home from her visit with you? Of course there is a difference, but that doesn't mean either form is worth less than the other. Young people, and increasingly people of all ages, listen to tapes. They've become part of our life just as books are.

✷ **Buying a tape recorder.**   There are cassette recorders of every size and description to fit every pocketbook. Probably you own one of more of these if you have a recent radio, and most radios are also cassette tape players. You don't need to spend a lot of money. The smaller ones are generally more expensive.

I bought a very serviceable handheld cassette recorder that I use frequently to interview. I did not want one with a radio or stereo in it because I wanted something lightweight and very portable. It weighs about two pounds, and the microphone is built in. I buy cassette tapes in quantity at a very low price. Each tape has a label on it, and the recorder has a counter so that I can log in where an interview begins.

Most recorders can run on batteries or be plugged in with a small converter. I use a lot of batteries whenever I interview because I don't want wires hanging around.

Some people are a little shy of the recorder at first. Occasionally I have met strangers who refused to allow me to tape them, but most people are willing and even eager once they get going. Most people love to talk about themselves and are flattered to be asked. Some years ago I asked my mother-in-law if I could interview her. She looked a little reluctant but didn't seem to know how to say no politely. She agreed to a session, and for the first few minutes she kept glancing uneasily at the small black box on the table in front of us as if it were going to explode. Then my wife and I started asking her about her girlhood, her days at college, and her early years on the family farm, and she chattered away happily and completely forgot about it, or so it seemed to us, until she nudged my wife and pointed to the machine, which had run out of tape. June put another tape in and we went on with the interview.

❊ Conducting an interview.   It helps to prepare some in advance, but I keep my notes unobtrusive and try not to consult them until very close to the end of the interview to see if there's something I've forgotten. I often prepare a lengthy list of questions and then set them aside. The more you can make the interview seem like a genuine conversation that just happens to be taped the better. Don't make a production of turning the machine on or off or of changing tapes. It's best if you can talk and do these things as you ask questions and listen to what the person has to say.

It may help to stimulate memory with photos or other memorabilia. A photograph gives the person being interviewed something specific to talk about and also takes attention away from the machine. The best thing you can do to get a good interview is to enjoy the conversation and get involved in it, but try hard to be a good, attentive listener—ask questions.

"You were a linotype operator?"

"Yes. Forty years."

"Forty years! That's a long time. Did you always use the same machine?"

"That's right. On the *Dispatch* I used the same machine from the day I walked in there until I retired in 1967."

"So you started as a linotype operator in 1927?"

"That's right."

"Tell me about linotype machines. They're noisy . . . and smelly too, aren't they?"

He laughs. "Well, yes. But I always liked my machine. I sat

at it all day long. It wasn't so noisy, not like a press.
They rattle away."
"What rattles?"
"Oh, all kinds of things."
"What smells?"
"The lead pot stinks a little. You get used to it."
"Lead? That's bad for you, isn't it?"
"Well, yes, that's what they say now. If I'd known I was go-
ing to live so long I probably wouldn't have worked
there." He laughs again.

I ask questions, some of which are rhetorical ("You did? What
did you say?") but I try to make most of them substantive so that the
person being interviewed will produce a good answer. Most people
are interesting, but it may take a skillful interviewer to get them to
show it. Don't become inquisitorial or investigative. They'll clam up
and you'll have a tape with a lot of silence on it. Think of yourself as
a facilitator, someone who opens doors and gently offers entrance
into some of the rooms of their past. A good interview is a guided
conversation.

Let the person being interviewed know what you intend to do
with the tape. Offer to make them a copy of it. Be sure to get permission from the person if you plan to use the tape publicly in any way.

Before you leave the room, tape a label onto the cassette and
write in the date, time, and person interviewed; the place; and possibly the subject matter. If you aren't demanding with yourself about
doing this before you leave the place of interview you may well end
up with a drawerful of unmarked tapes. You may even accidentally
erase one in order to record another.

If you interview several people at once in the same interview, be
sure you identify each person's voice on the tape. A group interview
can be a lot of fun, but you need to gently seek to avoid having them
all talk over each other in their excitement to tell about some memory.

If no one in the family is able to interview you, consider finding
an interview friend. This works beautifully for couples, who can reminisce together on tape with a few prearranged topics. Don't deter-
mine what you're going to say because you don't want the
reminiscence to sound like a script. It's important to be authentic and
spontaneous. You can also interview yourself. For some people this
doesn't work—the prohibition against talking to oneself just can't be
overcome. But others acclimate very easily and get a certain depth

and insight that they might not achieve if they were talking to someone else.

Interviews between parent and child or grandparent and grandchild are especially effective. Teachers often assign their young students to interview their elders about "the old days." Kids are naturally inquisitive, love stories, and may well have something important to say to you about their own lives. They also take to operating a cassette recorder as if they were born doing it. And I can't think of a better gift to give loving adult children who are also doting parents themselves.

☞ SUGGESTION:

Get your cassette recorder and a fresh tape together and interview the oldest member of your family you can conveniently get to in person. If you can get the youngest to interview the oldest, then you already have your next holiday gift all picked out.

Writing Captions

✳ Pictures generate words. One of the favorite times at our family reunions is when somebody brings out a handful of old photographs.

"Is that you, Grandma?" one of our sons asks. "Why, you had black hair."

"Oh, that was a long time ago," Grandma says, looking at the picture. "And that dress. I just loved it. I wore it everywhere."

"Where was that taken?"

"Oh, that was our little house on Miller Street. Dad had two beehives out back."

"Beehives? In Indianapolis? They allowed that?"

"Dear, it was 1925."

We all laugh.

Family photos do something like this in every family at every reunion. A picture may be worth a thousand words, but it also causes people to exchange several thousand more in reminiscing. That's why looking at them is an ideal way to write a family history. Writing about photos or other artifacts like diplomas or birth certificates is a wonderful way to begin writing family history because it is so accessible. What could be more natural? Looking at these things generates ideas. You simply write these ideas down.

Yet photo albums and scrapbooks, fascinating as they are, often raise more questions than they answer. As such, they are tangible invitations to write. You wonder who is in the picture with your father. Was that his friend Al, whom he used to talk about going to college with? Why are they all dressed up? What's happening or is about to happen? One question seems to lead to another.

Even more tantalizing in their silence are such artifacts as an athletic letter still in a cellophane packet, a pair of ticket stubs to a ballgame in Saint Louis (who went? who won?), or a blue ribbon that says First Place, Madison County Relays. These things invite questions. Perhaps in your generation there is a possibility of answers with a little research. But a generation further on, and no one will have the slightest idea—unless, of course, you write something to go with them.

In my family my mother wrote all over the pictures, and sometimes turned them over and wrote on the back too. Her beautiful handwriting told why the camera had cut off the head of somebody in the photo, whose dog was being scratched on the belly, or whose toy truck that was in the lower foreground. In doing this she made these photos into little snapshots of family history. Archivists turn pale at the thought of writing on a photo, but I'm sure glad she did it. The worst, most useless photo is the one of people no one recognizes.

If you don't know where to start writing, simply pick a favorite photo and write or type some text around it on a page. Then go to a copy shop and have the result laser color copied. I recommend doing this with all new photos as you have them developed.

One advantage of this system is it doesn't commit you to a huge project. A photo caption can be written in minutes and is a lot of fun. You can write as much or as little as you like. Naturally, your family will appreciate extensive details. Try to answer all the questions you think a grandchild or other family member not familiar with that photo might ask. If you do this with photos just back from the developer, then fifty years from now your descendants won't have to struggle to remember why you're all dressed up in that photo of you and your college pal.

When you look at the picture and write your caption, it may be very helpful to think of yourself simply as jotting down some notes. Don't try to be organized or even logical. If a memory pops into your head, put it down. Go for the spontaneous. It may turn out to be the most interesting detail. Even if you don't know something for certain, it may be the best policy to put that thought down and then add that you are unsure.

I showed my mother a photo of her and some friends of hers, that she hadn't seen in years (Fig. 3–1). I taped what she said to me in her living room that afternoon, and then I went home and wrote up the following caption, using her words almost verbatim. Notice how a narrative is generated quite naturally.

I had just turned eighteen. It was 1927 and I was a senior at Manual Training High School in Indianapolis. It was state tournament time in basketball. We never "ditched" class in those days—or at least I didn't—so school must have been out. They could have dismissed classes, but I doubt it. It might have been a Saturday.

We were just out having fun and this guy, a photographer from the *Indianapolis Times* said, "Hey, girls. Let me take your picture against the car."

I don't know whose car we're standing all over. It sure wasn't ours. It says "Beat Muncie" on the back windshield, but we probably didn't care who won. Or maybe an Indianapolis high school was playing Muncie and we did care. I don't remember.

Anyway, the photographer—we must have thought he was pretty cute or we wouldn't have done all this—got us to pose on the car, and he snapped the picture.

I'm the one in the center holding a streamer or something. My mama made that dress for me, a blue silk moire. (We didn't have synthetics like polyester or nylon in those days.) The sweater is probably a school sweater, and the tam-o'-shanter was red and white, my school colors.

The other girls are Evelyn Burns, on the far left, then Marie Vick and, on the far right, Betty Delph. Marie and I kept in touch for years, but I've lost track now.

The tournament was at the Butler University Fieldhouse. We'd go early in the morning on the streetcar and stay all day. Each year one of the high schools would run a lunchroom at the fieldhouse and we'd eat right there.

The last game was on Saturday night. Some people scalped tickets, but the authorities caught on and issued new tickets, so all the scalpers lost their money.

I enjoyed high school and did well in my classes. In fact I had the grades to be eligible for an honor student club but I

FIG. 3–1   *A photo like this from your album is a great starting point for writing family history.*

wasn't asked to join. I wasn't Jewish, but they thought I was because of my last name, "Isaacs." That's the way things were back then. There were a lot of Jewish kids at Manual High—there was a synagogue next door—but they couldn't be in the honor society.

There were lots of Negroes, too, and we thought nothing of it. But the next year, 1928, they built a new high school for them, Crispus Attucks, and the Negroes had to go to school there—no choice.

I knew John Dillinger. He was an Indianapolis hoodlum. I mean I knew who he was. He wasn't in high school but he was hanging around. His girlfriend was in one of my classes. She might have been the famous "woman in red" who later caused his capture. I knew Hoagy Carmichael, too. He lived across the alley from us.

Oh—what happened to the picture? It showed up next afternoon on the front page of the *Times*. Everybody kidded us about it and we all thought it was really funny.

The photo interview method is an excellent way to get history from someone too elderly or too busy to do any writing otherwise. Many older people simply can't believe that anyone would be interested enough to read their reminiscences and so won't go to the trouble of writing anything down. But they often will talk into a discreetly handled cassette recorder and be a delightful and interesting subject. And then, of course, you have the information about the photo and the additional treasure of a tape recording of the person talking about it.

This scrapbook approach to history, homemade as it might seem, isn't greatly different from what museums do. Most museums are little more than scrapbooks of artifacts. Near my home here in Kansas is the Eisenhower Museum in Abilene. What is it but a scrapbook that, had they had time and money, might have been put together by loving grandchildren? Here are Ike's school pictures, letters he wrote and received, and even his staff car—everything about his life that helps us understand his origins, his life and times, and his achievements. What if we were provided with that much information about our ancestors? Would our identity be stronger, our sense of where we came from greater, and our handle on the future firmer and surer? I can hardly doubt it.

It helps if the photo is intrinsically interesting. The charming photo in Fig. 3–2 brings a broad smile to faces old enough to remember that milk comes from a cow. Here are Lula Leverenz' recollections of her life then as she looked at that picture. Note how much background history she gives, and how the text is much, much more than a caption.

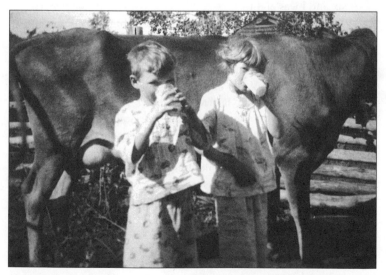

FIG. 3–2 *Lula Leverenz created a wonderful memoir of her childhood from this photo.*

Morning Eye-Opener
by Lula Leverenz

The summer of 1932 was in the heart of the Great Depression. In my father's quest to find work to support his little family, he also provided me with some of my greatest memories and pictures to go with them. He owned a folding Eastman Kodak camera and used it a lot. We were dirt poor, but Dad didn't spend money on tobacco or whiskey. He spent what little he could spare on film for his camera or a quart of hand-packed ice cream once in a while.

By the summer of 1932 he had ended his career as manager of a Conoco oil station at Delta, Colorado, and we moved to the mountains about thirty-five miles northeast. My dad worked the packstring in sheep camp, the packstring being the horses that packed in the supplies from the nearest town. There were no roads for cars or trucks, only trails for the horses. We took along a crate of Mama's chickens, our milk cow, our Boston bulldog Tony, Mama's rocking chair, the washtubs. All this paraphernalia was packed in by the horses, up the mountain, with the chickens squawking, the rocking chair and the washtubs bouncing and swaying, the cow docilely plodding along behind, and Tony as happy and carefree as my brother and I were. This was to be the most memorable summer of my life. Larry was six and I was eight.

We lived that summer in a log cabin that people hadn't lived in for a long time. Range cattle had pushed in the door and used it for a stable. One of the sheepherders who had helped pack us wouldn't get off his horse until Mama had seen the inside of the cabin. He expected that she would refuse to live there. But Mama didn't react that way, so Ralph got off his horse, got the scoop shovel and set to work helping get our new home cleaned out. It was cozy and clean when Mama was done with it.

Dad took pictures—pictures of the cabin, the packstring, Larry in his pajamas going for an early morning ride on his sawhorse "horse," me sweeping off the steps of the cabin and getting my hair washed outside under the trees, the sheep, our dog trying to catch the hornets, Pete the mule, and this one: Larry and me having our morning eye-opener, just out of bed and still in our pajamas. Many times, while Dad was milking our Jersey cow and as she was tied to the rail fence, we ran down with our cups to have a morning eye-opener.

Sheep camp was exactly that: lots of sheep grazing in the mountains, sheepherders living in tents, trusty sheep dogs to help them, a summer of new lambs, tail-docking time and the smell of citronella afterwards, walking through the beautiful landscape where the blue columbines bloomed. And listening to "When It's Springtime in the Rockies" played on a small, hand-wound phonograph owned by one of the sheepherders. It was probably the first and last time those sheepherders had their territory invaded by a woman and two kids. But I think it made their summer as enjoyable as ours, especially when they were in the vicinity of our cabin and were invited in for a meal, or when we took them a treat to where they were camping with sheep. One of them said to Mama, "Mrs. Russell, you shore can make good biscuits!"

A final example of an extended photo caption comes from my own family archives. The caption for this photo was actually a journal entry I made in 1980. This allowed me to present with real certainty the actual events that occasioned the photograph, one of our family's favorites.

Mother's Day, 1980

"Ben?"

"Hi, Dad."

"You're up early." We were standing in the hall outside the bathroom.

"Yeah." Ben walked quietly to the back door and slipped on his mother's garden clogs.

"What are you going to do outside?"

"I'm making a present for Mom."

I smiled and nodded. I watched him clomp back down the steps of the deck and head toward the creek. He turned around and suddenly came back.

"Dad," he said through the screen door, "don't let Mom get up yet. Okay?"

"Okay."

FIG. 3–3 *This photograph of the author's son invites the telling of a story.*

But our youngest son, Rip, had heard our talking, and now he was up too, slept out and hungry. He stood up in his crib and grinned.

"Hello, Ripper. Do you want some of Mom's milk?" I lifted him out and carried him into our bedroom. June, already awake, saw us. Sore and leaking milk, she was as eager to have Rip nurse as Rip was to do it.

"I'll get your tea," I said. I handed Rip over. He began sucking noisily.

When I came back with the tea I told her Ben didn't want her to get out of bed now.

June laughed. "May I go to the bathroom?"

"Better do it before Ben gets back."

"Where is Ben?"

I shrugged. "Big surprise." It would be a surprise to me, too. But I didn't tell her that.

She slipped out of bed and handed Rip to me. I sat down in the rattan chair in the corner and stood Rip on my knees. He held onto my thumbs. I leaned forward.

"Hy-drau-lic cyl-in-der," I intoned slowly. Rip squealed with delight at this game we both loved to play. Slowly and steadily I pulled him back and forth like this several times, each time repeating the words "hydraulic cylinder." He didn't take his eyes off me and he didn't stop grinning.

Until he saw his mother coming. Then he practically leaped for her.

June got back in bed. Rip nursed on the other breast. I got a cup of coffee. When I came back I sat down and read yesterday's newspaper. I smoked a cigarette. In a few minutes, I heard Ben at the door.

"Dad, open the door, will you?"

I let him in. "Oh," I said when I saw what he had made. "That is very nice."

"Is Mom awake?"

"Awake but in bed nursing your brother."

Ben slipped off the clogs and took his gift into the bedroom. I followed.

"Happy Mother's Day," he said, holding out the board.

The big mud letters said "MOM." Ben had laced the letters with tiny lavender blossoms from the lilac bush. In the center of the O he had put a seashell.

"Oh, Benny," June said, "thank you." She started to cry.

Ben set the board at the foot of the bed. He hugged his mother. "I love you, Mom," he said. I went over too, and kissed her forehead. Rip stopped nursing and looked up at us, smiling broadly. Clumsily we did a group hug.

"My three boys," June said. "My three boys."

These three examples suggest some of the possibilities of the form. For simplicity in getting started, nothing works better than looking at a family photo and jotting some of the recollections that it evokes. If writing about photos is not possible—as at a reunion, where so much is happening—bring out your tape recorder and show the photo (give each one a number so that you can match up the comments with the photo) and ask for comments. I guarantee that you won't have trouble getting people to talk.

☞ SUGGESTION:

Find your most recent batch of photographs. Put them in a stack on your writing desk. Number them consecutively on the back very lightly with a soft-lead pencil in the lower left-hand corner. Now write a caption, long or short, for each photo on a sheet of paper and put it next to the corresponding number.

Letters

When we sit down to write a letter to someone in our family, we are also writing history. Of course it's informal, off the cuff, and even random, but it is history nonetheless. I have in my possession a one-page letter from my great-grandfather to my grandfather. It is all I know of my great-grandfather, and it raises more questions than it answers.

> My Dear Son,
>
> I have been thinking about you ever since I came over here. I want to hear from you. How is your rheumatism by this time? I am doing quite well considering the condition I was in. I think I am gaining in strength though I can tell you I am not very strong yet. But I am teaching and earning my salary, and I mean to stick to it as long as I can. It was pretty hard at first and I had much headache the first week. I have just got in half a month. I have 31 pupils now. I got a letter from Lottie today and a card from Leon yesterday. I want to hear from you. I want to write to Will, soon. He is at business in Yankton.
>
> I think I can go home on Saturday and back on Sunday. I shall try it soon. Write me soon. Love to all
>
> > I remain
> > Your Loving father,
> > John Kempthorne

I reproduce the text of this letter here because, though it is a skimpy bit of family history, it still tells a lot about some very important things. My great-grandfather was a teacher and he was apparently dedicated. He was also a devoted father, a serious family man.

He seems to have been a simple, straightforward man: "I want to hear from you." These are important things to know about one's ancestors. And look how much can be learned from a single letter!

✳ Is letter-writing dying out?   We will always have letters. A certain percentage of the population likes to write and understands that you can do things in letters that you cannot do over the phone. It's not unusual to meet someone who loves to talk on the phone but will also write letters to the same people, usually to expand on topics covered in the conversation.

Letters permit that. They allow one to go on and on and be uninterrupted. There's no guarantee that a letter will be read in that fashion of course, but a good letter gets read, often several times. You can't do that on the phone. Letters also permit the writer to have a thought, write it, then think some more, and amplify or even change that thought.

So while the popular opinion is that letters as a form of writing are pretty much dead, it's not the whole story. Letter-writing has been going on throughout history. Even today we occasionally see in the news that a packet of letters between a prime minister and his lover or between one literary giant and another has been found. Everyone used to have a chest in the attic filled with old letters. Now our houses do not have attics, and we don't have very many letters to save either. That's a shame.

✳ Electronic letters.   We do have, however, email. Email, also sometimes written *e-mail*, is electronic mail sent from one computer to another via telephone lines. If you own a computer, then you can install an inexpensive device called a modem that allows you to hook up to your telephone line. You log onto your computer and dial the phone number for the local hookup with the Internet, a giant worldwide network of computers originally started for researchers and government organizations. Now all kinds of people use the Internet. Access is easy, quick, and cheap, or free. Even those of us who do not work for a large organization like a university or a huge corporation can sign up for a commercial service and for a few dollars a month have email capability.

Email allows people to send written messages back and forth almost instantaneously and without paying long-distance costs. Clearly, email has its own advantages and disadvantages. Most emailers feel they write less formally than in a letter. It is something like being down the hall from a colleague or chatting over the back fence with a neighbor. But of course it's writing and has all those advantages—the opportunity to restate and to reflect and the necessity to interpret and mull over the message.

❋ Letters as history.   The copier has made it still easier for letters to be used as history. Many people now make a copy on a copy machine of every letter they send. Often post offices will have copiers in their lobby, and you can hold your letter open until you go to the post office, make the copy, and then seal and mail it. And of course people still save letters—as they should. They will be part of the history of the future.

What about letters you have in the family in a closet, drawer, or shoebox? What should you do with them? You should make them available to other members of the family just as quickly as you can. Of course you don't want to part with the original letters and risk losing them. What I'm suggesting is reproduction and publication. This can be done very reasonably.

Let's say you have a packet of a dozen or so letters between your mother and your father, both of whom are now dead. Your four children may not even know about the letters—they weren't all that interested when they were young and you were too busy. Now your children are married and having children of their own and their thoughts turn, inevitably, to their feelings of being part of a process. Now they would be very interested, and you have the time to get things out there.

The simplest thing is to take the letters to a copy shop and make four copies of each one (make copies of the envelopes too, so the date and stamping can be seen), and then send a set to each child. An improved version that also makes sure the letters don't get misplaced would be to compile the letters into a book or booklet, which you can do at the copy shop as well. You might decide at that point to write a little preface about where you got the letters, the people mentioned, or other historical context that will make the letters more interesting. You might even want to sandwich in some comments of your own between letters. This may be absolutely necessary, in fact. Standing alone, the letters may not make a lot of sense. You may need to insert a comment that Sarah took ill shortly after receiving a letter from John proposing marriage, and that was why it took her two months to respond. Be careful, though, not to explain the obvious or to get in the way of the letters you want to showcase.

You might type the letters, leaving only one or two in script to give the flavor of the originals. You might want to put some photographs with them too. For example, in the letter John writes to Sarah about the new house he bought for them in Cleveland, you might have handy a photo of that house. As with so many family history projects, you can do a little or a lot, depending on your time, interest, and budget.

You may have only one or two letters, and you probably won't have the responses as well as the letters. You may have letters written by a relative stranger to your father or mother, or you may just have a miscellaneous collection of letters your mother received and didn't throw away. What you have will govern what you do in the way of publication, but do publish them. Letters are history that is firsthand and seen from the front row seat.

Not long ago an old school friend and I got in touch with each other after a lapse of many years. We had been best friends in high school though he was a year ahead of me. Tony sent me a small packet of letters that his mother, bless her, had saved among Tony's things—letters that I wrote to him as a senior in high school after he had graduated and joined the Air Force. These letters were a revelation to me. I had not seen them since I mailed them some forty years ago, and since I didn't keep a journal until I was in my late twenties, I had no written record of my mind—so to speak—and it was a little embarrassing to find out that I sounded like a teenager.

Another personal example concerns the time when my daughter went to live for a year in Greece after high school. Being a writerly sort of person, she sent me a number of letters and I responded. I saved copies of my letters and of course hers too. I'm going to let them simmer a few more years, maybe until she has children of her own, but someday I'm going to publish them for her and her husband and for their children . . . and their children.

☞ SUGGESTION:

Find a recent letter or letters from someone in your family or circle of friends with whom you've corresponded more or less frequently in the past. Clip that letter to a sheet of paper on which you have written an account of that correspondence—its frequency, use, and meaning or any other important characteristics. If you've had the foresight to save copies of your own response(s), clip that on too.

Occasional History: Cards and Letters

✳ Ready-made versus homemade cards.   The greeting card business has become a burgeoning and extremely successful business in the past generation or so. I love to get cards on my birthday as much as anyone, but it's a tad depressing to open the big, colorful and professional-looking card and just see a name signed under all the good wishes tendered in print to me and one million other folks whose friends and relatives have two bucks to spend on a card. While a store-bought card is not as depressing as an empty mailbox, I would rather get a homemade card. I know they take more time. But consider them as history too and as a chance to pleasantly reminisce.

✳ The get-well reminiscence.   The get-well card is an especially good time to consider making your own card (or folding a letter inside a store-bought card) because it is such a difficult and often sensitive situation. Chances are the recipient is tired of hearing about get-well wishes and would like to think about something else. That's the stance that Jean Burdakin took when she sent a card to a friend who was seriously ill. She wrote a sketch about a wonderful time both of them would remember and sent it to her friend:

Househunting and a Very Special Neighbor
by Jean Burdakin

"Moving to Pittsburgh, John? Uh-oh, someone in the company must have heard me say, 'I love living in Berwyn, Pennsylvania. I could stay here forever!'"

A number of people at work told John that the Fox Chapel suburb of Pittsburgh had excellent schools. So a few weeks later John and I looked at the few houses in the Fox Chapel area that were for sale in our price range.

In our moves, John, the pragmatic one, made sure there would be room in the house for the five of us while I noted which house had the prettiest yard. One house with a very lovely yard John thought would be a bit small but was willing to consider it. The real estate lady, having first phoned that we were coming, let us in. The lady of the house was seated on the sofa painting her nails bright red. A son in his late twenties smoked as he stared at us from his chair. The French poodle was friendly as we apologetically passed through the room—noting that the beige wall-to-wall carpet was a virtual sea of small yellow stains.

Exploring the house included a trip to the lower level. We passed through the washer-drier area and on into a long, narrow family room with small windows on the right side. At the end, John, the engineer, thought to himself: Why on earth do they have a closed drape in the middle of the inside wall? To satisfy his curiosity he pulled on the gismo that opened the drapes. Immediately he found himself at very close range with a life-size photographic enlargement of the nude, well-endowed upper body of the lady sitting on the sofa upstairs. The three of us laughed till the tears ran. Then we realized we had a problem. How were we going to pass back through the living room with our faces straight? We finally mastered enough self-control for a fast exit.

The house we actually bought had its own set of peculiarities. We detected a few problems as we looked at it. However it seemed fresh and clean, there was plenty of room for all of us, and it had a beautiful view.

A family of five isn't in a house very long without exploring the kitchen. Oh, no, we opened the cabinets to find a sea of . . . no, not small yellow stains, not goldfish, but mice droppings everywhere. In the pullout bread drawer the droppings were so thick we just pulled the whole thing out to replace with new. Undiluted Lysol had to do for the cabinets.

The doorbell rang and the delightful and welcoming neighbor, Pat Mansmann, who lived across the street, stopped in to meet the rest of us. She, Jack, and their seven children had already met John when he first looked at the house.

Pat rolled her eyes but wasn't that surprised about the mice. She told us that the lady who had lived there before us kept little night lights burning in the cabinets to keep the mice babies warm! However, Pat was incredulous when she saw all the white spaces on the walls where the furniture had been. "No wonder she was able to paint the whole inside in a few days," she exclaimed. "I wondered how she managed to do it so fast."

We were comfortably settled, the boys in school, when we noticed the water stain on the living room ceiling and watched it get larger whenever the tub upstairs emptied. I also asked Pat about the large black ants I kept seeing in the kitchen. She said they were carpenter ants—a problem when woods are near the house. One day I spotted one emerging from a hole in the door to the kitchen closet. I went over to look and heard a sound. Putting my ear against the hole in the door I heard the sound of Niagara Falls. (Really! I've been there.) I called to John, who removed the door and carried it out onto the roof of the carport and split it open with an ax while I sprayed Raid on the thousands of ants as they scurried out.

Would we have bought this house if we had known all these things? Oh, yes—a thousand times, yes!

What is one of the most priceless things in life? Friendship! Pat and I never had sisters. We became sisters for those three years we shared as very special buddies. She invited me to join her garden club. I soon found myself copying Pat as we together made and decorated teasel weed trees, prepared delicious grilled mushroom sandwiches for the large Shadyside benefit, as well as large papier-mache candle holders from bottles with interesting shapes. Yes, Pat is very creative. I soon became her number one fan and follower. She and I both loved to putz in our gardens. When we moved to Cleveland, Pat gave me lots of shoots for my memory garden. I still have her "Old Honesty" and "Fever Few" in my Michigan garden.

Whenever my three sons exasperated me, I headed over to Pat's for a glass of her iced tea. Pat had an enormous old pitcher which always seemed to be refilled. I hardly got to mention what was bothering me before realizing how unimportant it really was compared to raising seven children. Then I would become the listener instead. Somehow we always both felt better after our chats.

I would wish for everyone that they could have a friend, a neighbor, a good-buddy-like-a-sister like my Fox Chapel friend, Pat.

✳ **Birthdays and anniversaries.** Marriage anniversaries provide an opportunity and an occasion for family history that fits quite naturally with the event. It's very natural to look back after ten or twenty-five or more years. A booklet, a combination of photos and text, helps the family to do this. Such a booklet can basically become the story of a marriage and a brief family history. Matthew Figi, who wrote *Figi's Fiftieth*, a celebration of his family, honored his parents in 1992 by writing an account of their marriage and family life.

Filled with photos of family and documents, this twenty-page booklet is a simple, straightforward account presented as a narrative and filled with anecdotes. The need and the technology are there for this to be done in every family. It is hard to read this account of ordinary lives, marriage and honeymoon, children, illness, work, and the whole of life together and not be moved. The lives of the celebrated and extraordinary may astonish us, but the lives of ordinary people stir the soul.

Birthdays, of course, provide an excellent opportunity for a retrospective of a page or two of photos and text or even a whole booklet or book. One adult child might act as an editor of an anthology for an elderly parent's book.

❋ The annual holiday letter.　Christmas is a time that already has a long-established letter tradition, but Christmas letters have a deservedly bad reputation. If you are like most people when you get a Christmas letter from friends or relatives, you glance at it, read a line or two, and set it aside to plow through later. Perhaps your eyes fell on a line like "In April we were so proud when John was awarded Salesman of the Month by the District K-Mart Office, and then in May . . ."

Most such "annual" letters are not difficult to get through because the recipient doesn't like or isn't interested in the sender. The problem is these letters are summaries. This may be the one letter per year that the Joneses are sending out to these friends whom they love and want to keep in touch with, and so they want to convey all the news of the year: "In January, Sarah won an oratory contest; in February, Mom was in an auto accident; in March, Sammy went on a tour of Washington, D.C., with others in the seventh grade . . ."

Summaries in themselves are never interesting. This is hard to believe because we tend to believe that events are exciting. Often, however, events are not as interesting as their context; how and why they came to happen and what the feelings were of the actors can be very interesting matters.

This doesn't mean there's anything wrong with the idea of the Christmas letter. It's a great idea, but it hasn't been put to good use very often. The annual letter to friends is the perfect vehicle to give news, but it must be made interesting. The challenge is to get all the news in and still make the news a good read.

One technique is to break up the text with graphics and photos. Combining both is much simpler now with a computer than it was years ago. Another technique is to write a composite or even a

Marie, Cont'd.

Marie started high school in South Wayne. During her freshman year she was in the band and dated the captain of the football team. She was to spend the following summer (1942) in Chicago with Della Goddard and family. She got whooping cough and spent only one month there.

After returning home to Browntown, she met and fell in love with Dewayne Figi in August. In September she started back to school, but quit in January to get married.

Figis Married

Dewayne did his chores as usual in the morning

Tuesday, January 12, 1943 was a beautiful day, in spite of a large amount of snow and the temperature being 20 degrees below zero. In spite of the fact that it was his wedding day, Dewayne got up and did chores as usual in the morning. He was afraid his car, a 1935 Ford V-8, would not start due to the cold, but he was able to drive to Browntown to pick Marie up to go to the church.

Virgil drove the couple to the church parsonage in Browntown where he waited in the car while the couple was married. Leah Tomlinson, a neighbor of the Larsons, was one of the witnesses. She said that she "wishes that someone would have recorded the ceremony to play back years later" as the ceremony was so beautiful. Mrs. Haack was the other witness. Her husband performed the ceremony.

After the ceremony the trio went back down the street to the Larson home. Virgil took a picture of the couple outside the Larson house. Marie's mother prepared a nice oyster dinner for the newlyweds, Marie's parents and her brother Virgil.

After dinner the couple drove to Monroe where they had a formal portrait taken by Frautschy. The couple then travelled back to Browntown and took their luggage to the train station at the bottom of the hill. They took the car

6

FIG. 3–4   *Matthew Figi wrote and published this twenty-page booklet of the family's history on the occasion of his parents' fiftieth wedding anniversary.*

Jan 12, 1943

Browntown Girl and Local Boy Marry

The marriage of Miss Ida Marie Larson, daughter of Mr. and Mrs. C. M. Larson, Browntown, to De-Wayne Leonard Figi, son of Mr. and Mrs. Leonard Figi, Monroe, was performed at 1 o'clock this afternoon in the parsonage of the Evangelical and Reformed church of Peace, Browntown. Rev. J. L. Haack officiated.

An aqua dress of street-length and turf tan accessories was worn by the bride. Her corsage was of yellow roses. The couple was attended by Mrs. J. L. Haack and Miss E. Leah Tomlinson.

After the ceremony the newly-weds left immediately on a short wedding trip. They will reside with the groom's parents.

Mrs. Figi was graduated from Browntown state grade school and attended high school at South Wayne. Her husband was graduated from rural school.

Marie and Dewayne Figi on their wedding day, January 13, 1943.

back to the Larson home at the top of the hill.

After the couple went back down the hill, they boarded the train for their honeymoon in Waukesha. There was so much livestock on the train that it could hardly make it up the gradual grade to Monroe.

While registering in the hotel in Waukesha, a mouse ran across the floor. While on their honeymoon the couple dined twice with Marie's aunt Mary Johnson, sister-in-law of Marie's mother. Lars was to have joined them, but was sick in bed. Dewayne remembered so many forks and spoons, that he didn't know what to do.

When the couple returned to the Larson home in Browntown they found there was a blizzard. Dewayne's mother called to tell the kids not to chance driving to the farm. The couple was able to spend a couple nights with the Larsons.

After their return from the honeymoon, Marie's Sunday school class from Peace Church in Browntown gave the couple a shower. They received a white bedspread and two vanity lamps.

Dewayne remembered so many forks and spoons that he didn't know what to do

7

fantasy sketch of your whole family that conveys some of the feelings you've had that year. One person I know wrote a story about the family going to the woods on their farm to do the annual cutting of a tree to bring to the house and decorate. As the story progressed, he was able to unobtrusively put in bits of information about each member of the family. You might also consider writing a paragraph-long anecdote for each member and then putting the summary of events in a sidebar.

It helps to leave a space for a more personal message, something you can pen in. Generally speaking, if you make an effort to write the kind of letter you'd genuinely like to get yourself, your friends will enjoy it and be grateful for your touch.

☞ SUGGESTION:

Write a brief scene from the life of the next person you're going to send a greeting card to. Maybe it's a brother's birthday, a get-well card to someone, or an anniversary card to a couple you know. Fold the paper you wrote on (keeping a copy for your own historical archives), put it inside the card, and pop it in the mail. See what kind of response you get!

Cookbooks and Recipe Collections

One of the basic things families do is to prepare food and eat together. We all have memories of sitting around the family table. Some of these memories are happy, and some perhaps not. Some of the memories take the form of chuckles about each other's eating eccentricities. My grandfather ate peas with a knife, and his ability to load half a dozen green peas on the flat blade of the knife and get them into his mouth without dropping one was awe inspiring. My brother and I were both heavy milk drinkers, and my brother would refill his glass when it got half empty. He liked brown bread and raisin bread. I hated both. My father had the endearing habit of wanting a half piece of something—half a slice of bread, half a cup of coffee—and this became such a family joke that he started asking for quarters, eighths, and then sixteenths.

My mother, the cook, did not like to eat. She would cook the meal, sit at the kitchen side of the table, smoke a cigarette and watch us eat. Often she would give a running account of the cooking of the main dish or even of the entire meal. My memories of childhood are of all of us eating and occasionally looking up to see my mother watching all of us and talking. Every family has memories like that. Some families are talkative and happy at the table, some are quiet, even somber, but all have memories.

✳ Family recipes and family history: a natural mixture. It's a tradition also for families to pass on recipes. When my wife married me, her mother gave her a small index-card box filled with family recipes. Some of these recipes had a note or two, something like "Dad's favorite!" or "You loved this when you were a baby."

The idea of combining family history with recipes is nothing new, and it's so easy to make a cook- and history book now, there ought to be one in every family. That must have been in the mind of Elaine Hollabaugh when she wrote her beautiful book *A Taste of Honey*.

The book has a memoir and biography of her grandfather at the beginning. It's divided into sections—breakfasts, entrees, soups, salads, and so on. Nearly every recipe has some family history with it. Photographs of family members are scattered throughout, and at the end of the book is a list of all the members of the family, where they live and what they're doing.

Many loving parents have made cookbooks for their children by hand, too. Betty and Bob Watson of Minneapolis, Minnesota, have four daughters, for whom they created *The Four Sisters Cookbook*, filled with family history and recipes, each typed carefully and put in a leather three-ring notebook binder. The family history here is directly related to the recipe. It's fun if the recipe is in some way related to the history—the favorite food of the person whose biography is related, for example, or an incident that led to the acquisition of the recipe—but that doesn't have to be the case.

A cookbook is written one page at a time. That's what makes this kind of family history so accessible. And since you are typing up a recipe anyway, why not put a little history with it? That was the logic behind an assignment I gave my subscribers in an issue of *LifeStory* in which I asked them to send in a favorite family recipe along with some family history. Here's what Ardene Schneider Neve of Prior Lake, Minnesota, sent in:

The weekly trips to town for shopping were a highlight of the week. When Grandma's box of groceries included a picture-perfect aromatic California lemon, we knew our favorite—lemon pie—would be a dessert one of the days that

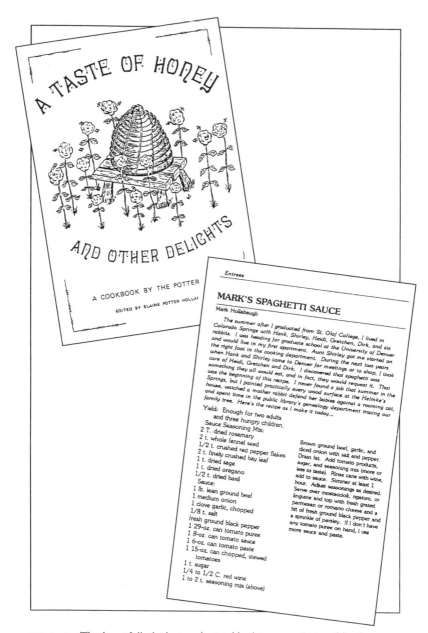

A TASTE OF HONEY

AND OTHER DELIGHTS

A COOKBOOK BY THE POTTER

EDITED BY ELAINE POTTER HOLLA

Entrees

MARK'S SPAGHETTI SAUCE

Mark Hollabaugh

The summer after I graduated from St. Olaf College, I lived in Colorado Springs with Hank, Shirley, Heidi, Gretchen, Dirk, and six rabbits. I was heading for graduate school at the University of Denver and would live in my first apartment. Aunt Shirley got me started on the right foot in the cooking department. During the next two years when Hank and Shirley came to Denver for meetings or to shop, I took care of Heidi, Gretchen and Dirk. I discovered that spaghetti was something they all would eat, and in fact, they would request it. That was the beginning of this recipe. I never found a job that summer in the Springs, but I painted practically every wood surface at the Helmke's house, watched a mother rabbit defend her babies against a roaming cat, and spent time in the public library's genealogy department tracing our family tree. Here's the recipe as I make it today...

Yield: Enough for two adults
and three hungry children.
Sauce Seasoning Mix:
2 T. dried rosemary
2 t. whole fennel seed
1/2 t. crushed red pepper flakes
2 t. finely crushed bay leaf
1 t. dried sage
1 t. dried oregano
1/2 t. dried basil
Sauce:
1 lb. lean ground beef
1 medium onion
1 clove garlic, chopped
1/8 t. salt
fresh ground black pepper
1 29-oz. can tomato puree
1 8-oz. can tomato sauce
1 6-oz. can tomato paste
1 15-oz. can chopped, stewed
   tomatoes
1 t. sugar
1/4 to 1/2 C. red wine
1 to 2 t. seasoning mix (above)

Brown ground beef, garlic, and diced onion with salt and pepper. Drain fat. Add tomato products, sugar, and seasoning mix (more or less to taste). Rinse cans with wine, add to sauce. Simmer at least 1 hour. Adjust seasonings as desired. Serve over mostaccioli, rigatoni, or linguine and top with fresh grated parmesan or romano cheese and a bit of fresh ground black pepper and a sprinkle of parsley. If I don't have any tomato puree on hand, I use more sauce and paste.

FIG. 3–5 *This beautifully laid out and printed book is a compilation of family history and recipes.*

week! She would have made a special trip to Nathan Gendler's small grocery store on Kob's Corner because Gendler's always had the choicest fresh produce. The Schneiders just plain liked lemon. In fact, in Aunt Allie's book *Reminiscing*, she tells of Grandma's starting a lemon tree in her house. One night an unfamiliar thump awoke Grandma and Grandpa. The mystery was solved the next morning when a plump lemon was found on the floor. It had become too heavy for the house-grown branch and had dropped to the floor with a thud.

But to get back to the pie: I remember her lemon pie from age three or four because she would let me roll the lemon in my hands. "Cuddling the lemon will help it give more juice," she said.

I watched her deftly roll out pie crust on the enameled pullout shelf of her "granny cupboard." She would save the last few "crimps" in the crust for me to complete. "First, wash your hands thoroughly, and then spread your thumb and first finger evenly and carefully so that the scallops around the crust are even," she would admonish. Into the oven would go the pie crust.

The next step would be to make the filling. She would hold me so that I might have a turn at stirring the fragrant lemon as it thickened crystal clear. "Always make a figure eight when you stir so your filling never burns tight on the bottom of your pan," she said, illustrating what a figure eight was. (I use the figure-eight stirring method to this day, sixty-some years later!) I loved watching the mounds of lemon dollop into the baked pie crust and then smooth out to the very edges.

The crowning finish was the meringue. The oven temperature in the cook stove was tested by opening the oven door and looking in. Since our farm was electrified by a Delco generating plant, electricity was not wasted on kitchen appliances. The primary uses of electricity were for the milking machines, grinding feed for the livestock, and pumping an adequate water supply if the windmill had failed to do so. Energetically, Grandma would turn the rotary egg beater until its whirring produced mounds of egg white. "A wee pinch of cream of tartar helps," she shared.

Grandma's lemon pie was admired and enjoyed by all

our relatives, neighbors, and the threshers whose annual rounds included meals at Grandma's.

When my dad and aunt dismantled Grandma's effects, they gave me the spiralbound recipe book I remembered from childhood. Imagine my delight and gratitude! The first thing I looked for was the recipe for lemon pie. I found it! In her neat precise handwriting appeared this recipe for lemon pie . . .

She follows this with a list of ingredients and then closes out the recipe/history with this little gem of family history:

Years later, a spectacular lemon tree flourished in my sister's California yard. Whenever she visited Minnesota, much to her children's humiliation, lemons were crammed into the nooks and crannies of their luggage to share with the family. I stated I would try to make a lemon pie like Grandma's. Although it was appreciated, in no way did it approach Grandma's luscious treat. In 1991, returning from our niece's wedding in California, we were able to stuff forty-eight into our luggage to divide among our family. I saved enough for our large family reunion when I baked six lemon pies. Relatives remembered Grandma's lemon pie, but all were kind enough not to make a comparison to mine . . .

Wouldn't it be rewarding if my grandchildren remembered my lemon pie made from Aunt Carolyn's California lemons with the same fondness that I remember Grandma's?

☞ SUGGESTION:

On a sheet of paper make a table with the following headings and fill it in:

FAMILY MEMBER	FAVORITE FAMILY RECIPE	REACTIONS (VERBAL, GUSTATORY, ETC.)

Biography

Most of us can write a biography of either or both parents without a lot of research. Many of us have access to enough research material to write biographies of grandparents as well as cousins, brothers and sisters, children, and friends. Biographies can be short or long or

somewhere in between. They can be rich in specific data and author-
itative or based mostly on some imaginative inferences. The subjects
of a biography can be deceased or still living and actively cooperat-
ing in the writing of their life.

Perhaps the biographer has access to all kinds of materials such
as letters, diaries, and other memorabilia and interview possibilities
with others who knew the subject. Just as often the biographer lives
in Missoula, Montana, and most of the family records (if they exist at
all any more) are in New Jersey.

✳ **Keep a research log.**   If you keep a journal, use it to carry on a
continuing dialogue with yourself about what you are doing so your
research will not be lost if anything happens to you. Notes stored in
a shoebox may reflect extensive research, but too often these are
found by not-very-interested heirs and thrown out as being of no
consequence. Every time you do some research, write the information up that day as fully as possible, in more or less coherent narrative form.

For example, at the end of a research session, you might write
something like this:

> I phoned Uncle Ernie today about that year that he and
> Dad spent together in the Army. He told me about the time
> they went on leave together and when they returned they
> discovered that their outfit had boarded a ship and was sail-
> ing out of New York harbor. "They're going to shoot us at
> sunrise," he remembers Dad saying, as they watched the
> ship, now half a mile away. "We were both scared," Ernie re-
> membered, "but I kind of thought, 'Well, it wasn't our fault
> the telegram didn't get to us,' and as it turned out the Army
> flew us ahead and we got to our duty station in time to meet
> the other guys as they came off the ship." "We missed our
> chance to get seasick," Dad told Ernie.

Notes like this, if kept in a spiral notebook, aren't likely to get
thrown out. Nor are you likely to puzzle over them, wondering what
they refer to. And of course this is reasonably good biography—if
only a tidbit—as it stands. If both you and Ernie died the next day,
there would still be this glimpse into your father's life.

✳ **Starting with a chronology.**   Take a sheet of paper and put a
date on one side and the event on the other. Include as much detail
as you have:

Feb. 11, 1904   Born in Chicago, 4th child of a streetcar conductor and his wife. Lived on Drexel Avenue near old Methodist Church. Father died later that same year.

Do this with every date you have in your subject's life. Don't be deterred by not having exact dates or places or sketchy details. Do the best you can with what you've got and note when you're not sure. That uncertain date or place or friend's name may become certain later; if it doesn't, then you can in your final write-up say simply that you are not sure.

The point of this chronology is to get some dates to measure other things by, to generate a list of possible scenes, to jog your memory, and of course to organize your research. Depending on the length of your biography, this could take several hours or several days and run from a couple of pages up to a dozen or even more.

❋ Establishing the scope of the biography.   Another outgrowth of the chronology-making will be a firmer understanding of your attitude toward this person. Probably you had strong feelings about your subject before you started, and this work will reinforce them. Grandpa was a loner, for example, or held many jobs that never mattered very much to him, and were just ways of earning the money to put food on the table; his "career" was being a woodsman and hunter. Listing your attitudes and focusing them will help you decide what kind of biography you want to write.

If you knew the subject, you might begin by writing a narrative memoir about your life with that person. The advantage of such an essay is that once again you are the expert because you are talking about your perceptions and feelings. You will be starting off on sure ground. Such a memoir might become the basis for a biography. Then if you can and want to, add a chronology, some memoirs by others close to the subject that you've gathered, and some documentation—photos or diplomas, for instance—and that may well be your biography. If you are writing a parent biography and some of your parent's siblings are still living, it would certainly be important to get taped or written memoirs if that is possible. But finally, the scope of the biography is up to you and should not be decided merely by the amount of material you have.

Like an autobiography, a biography can be a collection of material—letters, photos with captions (the more detailed the better), transcriptions of taped interviews with relatives and friends, memoirs by others, a chronology, documents like diplomas and awards, and so on. This "scrapbook" approach is absolutely sound biographically, even among those professional biographers who are writing lives of the great and famous. The point is, you are trying to write a biography that tells the reader about the life of the person in question: who he was, what she did, how he felt, what she thought, who his friends were, and what she loved and hated. You are telling the story of a human being.

These ventures are nearly always done without the prospect of a profit and often at the direct or indirect opposition of relatives (they fear what you'll say about them). Typically this history is written on evenings and weekends while you work full time, raise family, and do all the things that people must do to live. It is very, very easy to give up or procrastinate. It might be wise, then, to make the task as un-daunting as possible.

✳ A biography can be a few lines or ten thousand. Early on you will want to tentatively decide how long you want the biography to be. This decision can change as you discover you have more material or time than you thought. All of the following are biographies:

> My grandmother saved everything. In her basement, after Grandpa died, she stored everything, it seemed, that they had ever had—toys they had as children and that their own children had used, small hand tools from the farm, tons of clothes. Grandma wouldn't throw anything away. She had a mountain of rubber bands that she kept in a bowl by the front door—each day's newspaper brought a new one—and it worried her that she couldn't seem to find enough ways to reuse them. But she wouldn't throw them away.

> Lewis Clinton Isaacs was born in 1870 in Kentucky and died in Kansas in 1950.

> Gramps used to hold me on his lap and bounce me gently up and down by tapping his feet to the beat of poetry he would recite.

I'm overstating a bit here; of course a biography should be longer than the above examples, if possible, but it may not be possible. A reasonable biography of a grandparent could be one page long—about five hundred words and a photo or two. A biography of a parent could be half a dozen pages and as many photos. Material that comes in too late to be reasonably included in the main text can be added in footnotes, appendices, or even sidebars.

✳ Writing biography through scenes. Since often the problem in writing biography is not so much "how to" as "when to," it is worthwhile to point out that the most efficient means of writing a biography is to simply write scenes from the subject's life. The unpaid family historians, doing the work in their spare time, may not have the luxury of taking a year off to research and write an exhaustive biography.

A single narrative scene can say a great deal, anyway. If it is a typical scene it can lead us right to an understanding of the subject. And the purpose of a biography after all is to reveal character and not merely to number the days of someone's life. You might begin with a single image of your mother standing over the stove at six o'clock in the morning. Make a composite scene of a typical morning when you were in high school and your mother was busy getting you washed, fed, off to school, and launched into a successful and happy life.

Or you may choose simply to make "I remember" scenes (which may or may not be composites) in which you use little more than your own recollections and so are on firm ground: you don't have to worry about any facts but those of your own memory. Perhaps you remember vividly coming home from school. Your mother has been baking, and you and your sister come in. Mom has just taken out the pies and is coiling the little dough trimmings from the pie crust, dousing them with sugar and cinnamon, and putting them in to bake while you and your sister sit there, mouths watering, glasses of milk at the ready, waiting to eat the little "snails" (that's what my mom called them), and in the meantime telling her about the day at school.

Show Mom in the kitchen fussing about a button you lost on your school clothes or putting you to work cleaning your room. It's especially important to work some of her actual speech into the scene because what we say is often a revelation of what we are like. Of course you can't remember her exact words on that particular day, but that's not important. Have her say what she might have said then, saying you'd better have some homework in math to do this evening or she'd know the reason why.

✳ Building a biography from interviews. If the subject of your biography is still living, it's very important to get as much of that person on tape as you can if that's practical. Just as a series of scenes might constitute an excellent and thorough biography, but so also could a series of half hour- to hour-long sessions, possibly dealing systematically with the subject's life. If your subject feels like talking about her first job and it's the tape when you're supposed to find out about her trip to Europe thirty years later, then so be it. In family history, you make do—that is the only rule.

Larry Martz sent me a book of eighty-five pages he put together about his grandfather called simply *Recollections*. He flew to Chicago over a long weekend and taped four hours of his grandfather's reminiscences. His grandfather has since passed away. The concept of the book is simple. It's divided into "chapters" of varying length, usually one or two pages. Most of the chapters are a single anecdote directly transcribed from the cassette recorder Larry used. They have descriptive titles like "Chicago Racetracks" and "How Grandpa Was Hired by the Army."

They are wonderful anecdotes partly because Larry succeeded in getting his grandfather in a relaxed, reminiscent mood. His grandfather was an extremely interesting man, an automotive engineer who worked directly for Henry Ford and who was responsible in part for the fact that the American jeeps were so very well made. Many of the anecdotes are about his automotive work, but some are stories of everyday life. Just one will give an idea of the method and substance of this fine biography.

Grandpa Gets Robbed
by Larry Martz

I'll never forget it. One night, I was alone, and I went in my car to have a drink, and just as I sat down, I happened to remember that I'd forgotten to turn out my lights. In those days, you had to crank the cars by hand, and if you left the lights on, your battery would burn down, and then you wouldn't be able to start. So I got up to go out and see if my lights were out, and I was leanin' over, lookin' into my dashboard. When I straightened up, a guy hit me right in the head, and the next thing I knew, I woke up, and I was in a car with three other men. And they took me way out on the South Side, and they pulled over on this street, and they said, "What have you got on you?" At that time, I had this ring, right here, this diamond ring here. I'd just got it. And while I'm sittin' there, I didn't do nothing when they said that, I just set. But I kept workin' that ring off, workin' it off, and I finally got it in my hand, and I kept my hand closed around it 'till I got my hand in my pocket, and I dropped it in my pocket. And then, I gave 'em my money, probably fifteen dollars, it was a lot of dough, I'd just been paid that day, so it was a lot of money. I gave 'em the fifteen dollars, and then they argued among themselves if I should be beat up or not. And they did it openly to me. But they didn't do it; they finally let me go, and I know afterwards I hollered after 'em, "The least you could do is give me a nickel for car fare back to my car!" because they took me in their car. And a guy came back and threw a nickel at me.

This is a particularly good way to do a biography of an aged relative or friend in a short time. One of the hardest parts, I am sure, was the transcription itself. This is tedious work, even if you use a transcribing machine that allows you to operate the recording with a footpedal while you listen with earphones, leaving your fingers free to type. The future may allow a voice-activated typewriter to do all this for you, but for now this is the only way to achieve precise transcription. It works well for a short book to be published all by itself as Mr. Martz did or as part of a larger work with a chronology, documentation, and so on.

❋ Indicate when you aren't sure of your facts. What you say about your mother or father or grandparent will in all likelihood be taken as gospel and "become" that person for future generations of your family. Your words in a sense become a life. It behooves you, then, to be careful about your facts. This doesn't mean don't write a biography—who else will do it if not you?—but hesitate to be certain and don't hesitate to say when you're not.

In a journal, autobiography, or letter collection of your own letters, you are the authority on yourself. No one knows better what happened, was thought, and was said than you. It's your life, and if you say you felt like running away from home when you were fifteen, who can argue with that? But if you say the same thing about your father in a biography, you can be sure your brothers and sisters and mother and father will have their own thoughts. You will have to do research, and you will have to justify your interpretation of facts—and you will have to tell the reader pointblank when you do not know.

This isn't hard, but it does take a little getting used to. Document as much as you can. At the same time, don't be afraid to use your imagination based on the facts you know to dramatize your subject. A biographer can use lots of different tentative phrases.

Dad's dad was a blacksmith. Beginning about 1913 *I imagine* Dad spent a lot of time after school and on weekends in the blacksmith shop just off Main Street, a large building with glass windows at the front and huge wooden doors that could be swung open to accommodate horses and vehicles. The building was empty and the windows broken out when I saw it in the late 1940s. I remember very well Dad talking about shoeing horses. *I can easily imagine him in the shop, a handsome young high school boy almost a man, his schoolbooks sitting on a cluttered desk at the front, going about his father's business with hammer and tongs, listening to the clutch of loafers sitting around the big wood stove.* Someone in the family told me, *I think,* that Granddad, known as G. R., would at the drop of a hat close the doors of the blacksmith shop and go down to the Pecatonica River to fish. *If G. R. was like other tradesmen and shopkeepers of the time,* he almost certainly did a lot of work for the area farmers in exchange for food—a few dozen eggs, a ham, some fresh cream or butter. Dad always said G. R. never laid a hand on him or any of his five brothers and sisters. *I suppose* that what physical discipline was administered was done by their mother, and I'm *almost certain* that would be very little. *To the best of my recollection* I never heard Dad or any of my three uncles or two aunts say one bad word about their parents.

It might be useful to compile a list of tentative phrases and tack it up on the wall behind your writing desk. There will be many decisions about what to leave out and what to put in, but don't miss a chance to re-create the times because you are not dead certain of every fact.

❋ What about negative things? The person you are writing about must be believeable. You must present the character honestly. When writing about loved ones, the tendency for most of us is to leave out the warts, the "other" side they occasionally or even more than occasionally showed. Maybe your loved one—parent, spouse, child—had or has wonderful qualities mixed with not-so-wonderful qualities. How much do you tell?

I don't have an easy answer. Complexity is not an insurmountable problem, however. Sometimes biographers seem to be afraid that if readers are presented with the same facts that the author was presented with, the readers will reach a different, oversimple and erroneous conclusion. Maybe your father was a poor provider and the town drunk but a great hands-on father who taught you how to bait a fishhook, hit a baseball, and tell a joke so everyone would laugh. Most readers are discriminating enough to figure out the complexities and contradictions present in all human beings.

☞ SUGGESTION:

Write a biographical scene from your mother's or father's life that is representative of her or his adult life when you were growing up. You might choose a scene of your father at work shoeing horses and sharpening plowshares in his blacksmith shop, for example, or one of your mother doing the weekly shopping or baking bread. Keep it brief, only a page or two, so that you can write it easily in one sitting.

Autobiography

Writing an autobiography is not for everybody. Some people don't like to write or even talk about themselves. I would hope if you're doing a family history you will to some extent be autobiographical—after all, you're part of the family too. It is not vain to write about yourself. Your readers will be glad you did. And you can do the job better than anyone else.

On the other hand, a substantial number of family historians are primarily interested in writing an autobiography. They may feel that theirs is the only life they can write about with any degree of certainty. Or they may be writing in order to understand or to review their life and come to some conclusions about what it has been like so far. You may even feel that a sustained study of your life might be instructive for you or your readers—your children and grandchildren in most cases. Autobiography may be just the thing for you.

The form is almost infinite and various, as a reading of even a few autobiographies will show. You may find it useful to read a few by people you admire or feel some affinity with.

❋ **Let your autobiography take shape naturally.** Rather than trying to fit yourself into somebody else's idea of the proper autobiographical form, spend a few days or weeks thinking about yourself and who you are and let the autobiography take shape in order to reflect those conclusions. It might be worthwhile to do a little exploratory drilling into your life. How do you feel about this life you've lived? Has it been funny or tragic? Do you feel you've been held back or victimized in some sense? Have you led an orderly, methodical, and carefully planned life, and have things turned out pretty much the way you figured they would?

One way to get started thinking about structuring your autobiography is to make a chronology of your life that is more or less detailed and several pages long. Take a couple of hours to do it. This chronology is useful to get the data straight (did you move to Montana in 1937 or 1938?) and to get you to systematically review your life.

Another useful activity to prepare for writing an autobiography is to go through your photo collection and gather from ten to fifty photos of yourself, more or less evenly distributed throughout your life. Spread these out in front of you on a table or, better yet, pin them up on the wall in sequence. Now make notes just as you did on your chronology form. It might be a good idea to go down to the copy shop and get a color laser copy of each photo, cut them out, and paste each one on a separate sheet of paper that you make notes on. The idea here is to let the form of the autobiography grow out of the form of your life.

* **Your life as a series of scenes.**   List your friends chronologically on a page. Next, list the houses and towns you've lived in, the jobs you've had, the schools, and so on. These lists are excellent memory joggers, and the more notes you can make about each item the better. A list with notes is a kind of first draft of your autobiography. Also, as you compile these notes, the form of your autobiography is taking shape too.

It's also helpful at this point to make a list of "epitome" scenes from your life. Think of yourself as a screenwriter assigned the task of writing the story of your life. The worst thing you can do in an autobiography is to only summarize your life. You'll produce a more interesting (and more fun to write) autobiography if you select scenes for more or less full development and think of the summary as continuity connecting the scenes.

What scene comes to mind when you think of your grade-school years? One of mine is standing in between two other boys who are throwing my cap back and forth as I leap for it. Another is being in the schoolroom in the front row waving my hand and even snapping my fingers to get called on after the class has been asked

LifeStory Workshops

Chronology of Events and/or Representative Scenes

in the Life of _____

Date	Event	Comment

FIG. 3–6 *Forms like this can be very useful in getting the family historian started thinking and writing about her life.*

some question or other by the teacher; the very same boy who masterminded keeping my cap away from me is now staring sullenly at the floor while the teacher probes his lamentably thin storehouse of information. Probably the scene or scenes that come to mind will in fact be representative or will be of such importance (like the death of a parent or sibling) that they will need to be presented anyway. Ten or fifteen such scenes (depending on how old you are) fully developed could be an autobiography.

✳ The meanings of your life.   Another way to think about your life before beginning the autobiography is to think of your life as a plot. Many novelists let the plot of a novel grow largely out of the characters in it. What they do is the result of the kind of people they are. This may not be entirely true even for a novel much less real life, but it's useful to think about your own life in that way. Things happened to you, but to what degree did your own character make them happen? Possibly your character influenced your actions a lot, but it's also likely that the world impinged on your character. This process is just a way of thinking about your life in order to develop some focus to your narrative. Other ways include considering what you would do differently if you had your life to live over, what you would do more of, or what you think about your life is instructive.

If I am to judge from my own experience, most parents think about what they want their children to learn from the example of their own lives. And not all of these examples will be positive. You might want your children to learn a bitter lesson that you had to learn yourself from actual experience, and an autobiography is your chance to offer them some virtual experience of the bitter lesson that you learned.

I suggest that you make a list of what you find instructive and/or interesting about your life. This might be something fairly straightforward and simple like your youth as an explorer in the Himalayan Mountains. Or it might be something more complicated, such as the fact that you came back to your hometown later on and settled down into the family banking business and found a vastly more interesting world inside your own head or in the bank than the broadest vista from a mountaintop could ever be.

Remember that this is your chance to set the record straight, go into whatever detail you think is necessary for your life to be understood and appreciated, and reach out to others and tell them what you have found meaningful in life.

✳ Writing a summary autobiography first.   After you've done this listing and reviewing, you're ready to sit down and write a summary autobiography of a dozen pages or so. Again, do not think or try to organize much of this beforehand, just sit down and see what comes out. If you find that you've written a dozen pages and ten of them were about the five years you were a miner in the Yukon, then you will know that you should give a lot of attention to that period of your life. That may be the material that excites you enough into writing meaningfully about it. I know a man of sixty who has been working several years writing about the first twenty-five years of his life and has generated some excellent material. Better to write passionately and happily and well about one year than dutifully and ploddingly about sixty.

After you've written your summary on a separate sheet of paper, write a one-paragraph statement of what you would like your readers to understand about your life as a result of reading your autobiography.

✳ Telling the truth.　Many people fail to be honest in their autobiography, and honesty is the one trait you cannot do without. If the reader senses that you have written a "puff piece" to cast your life in the best light, even your own children will have trouble plowing through it, and they may reach conclusions that you don't want them to.

If on the other hand you are honest and willing to discuss some of your misjudgments and mistakes, then much else in the book will be forgiven. People think the essential ingredient in good writing is skill with words. It is not. The essential ingredient is being genuine.

This doesn't mean your autobiography must necessarily be a confession, but it does mean that you should tell the truth about what you take up. It is certainly acceptable to not tell about your errant youth, but don't lie and say you sang in the church choir and graduated summa cum laude if you didn't.

✳ Do it your own way.　You might want to write a few scenes from your life and then put them with a collection of letters you wrote, some photos with your commentary on them, and a chronology that's mostly data. That's okay. I don't want to say anything that might deter you from experimenting and inventing your own form that fits you best.

Remember that an autobiography is a unique chance to speak to the future. Think of that future. It's the year 2100 and you've been dead for a hundred years. What can you say to these people about your life that they can use in theirs?

☛ SUGGESTION:

Write a one-page biographical scene from your own life. Choose a scene that is representative of a certain period of your life—when you were a college student, say, or when you first got married.

The Family Newsletter

❋ The letter to the whole family.   A family newsletter might begin modestly as a letter from you to the rest of your family. This form was used for years by making carbon copies of one letter and sending one copy to each member of the family. Doing this was a great saving of time over everyone writing letters to everyone else and asking, "Did I tell you about Suzie's scholarship to Michigan State?" There was also the opportunity to address the entire family as if they were assembled around the kitchen table, even if all the members were scattered all over the country.

Copying machines have made these letters simpler and more interesting. You can make carbon copies of the letter or go to the copy shop and have them make the copies for you. A clear, sharp color copy of a photograph—just about as good as the original—would be a great addition. Then you can write to all your family and refer to a photograph by simply placing the photo on the page and writing your text around it. Pictures make letters more interesting of course, and family photos are history too. But that history is not getting used stuck in some photo album on the closet shelf. This sort of letter gets it out there.

Though these laser color copies generally cost about a dollar a page, that's not a lot of money. Certainly it's cheaper than taking the photo to a developer to make prints from the negative or the print itself.

❋ Round-robin letters.   I should mention also, if only as a kind of nostalgic epitaph, the practice of families sending "round robin" letters. A few families still do. In a common variation, one person—usually the parents—writes a letter and sends it on to another family member, who adds a page or so and then sends it on to the next, and so on until the letter comes back to Mom and Dad who file it away and send on another one. The great advantage of the round robin is that everyone gets to add their news and commentary.

The only problem is that if one member is late or absent minded enough to mislay the letter, then the whole thing breaks down. Follow-up letters have to be written or phone calls made to wake up the offending member.

❋ A newsletter for the whole family.   A family newsletter usually refers to the extended and not just the nuclear family. It's perfectly possible to have a family newsletter for a nuclear family, but if you're

Oines News
no. 1

OcT. 27, 1994
Photo of the Month

This is a special picture I am sure you will enjoy having, because the youngest child is your father — Henry Benard Oines.

It must have been around Christmas Time. Your father would have been nine months old. The oldest boy is his brother, Arthur Ingvald who died of the flu during a World War I flu Epidemic. He must have be 12 on this picture. Sister Ruth is 8. She died of a mastoid infection 1912. Oral must have been 5 on this picture. He died in an automobile accident.

Their shoes look shiny new. Isn't this a precious picture?

Dear Ron, Robert and Roger,
   Dad and I are beginning to feel at home in the Condominium in Fountain of the Sun in Mesa, AZ. We have two bedrooms and two baths, so we welcome family visits.
   We flew down to Phoenix two weeks ago. Ron and Myrna drove the car from Omaha. They stayed a couple of days then flew home to Tulsa. They helped us settle in. Thank you, thank you.
   This "photo" idea is a new project of mine. Hope it lasts.
   Arthritis is causing pain in dad's legs and shoulders. He misses his daily walks, but enjoys football games on TV.
   We have a dinner out once a day, so meals are no problem.
   Epiphany Lutheran Church is 8 miles from FOS, but we do feel at home there, so continue to drive to Apache Jct. weekly.

   Dad says, "Hi!"
                              Love and Blessings,
                              Mother

FIG. 3–7   *Margaret Oines' letter to her three children combines family history with a letter telling about the present. The laser copy of the family photo is almost as good as the original.*

going to go to the trouble of putting together a whole newsletter, then you're more likely to distribute it to your larger, extended family, probably somewhere between fifty and one hundred persons or even more. You can define family any way you want; but it may be best to keep the definition at first fairly narrow. Then in a single issue you can give a little news from each segment of the family and everyone will be interested. You can steadily expand as your own interest and proficiency grows, but try to include news and history of every branch in every issue

A newsletter goes beyond writing and publishing family history: it chronicles family history, recording the births, deaths, illnesses, ups and downs, retirements, and graduations of your family's life.

Remember that your newsletter should not be a promotional tool for some members of the family or a scandal sheet either. Your object is to give your family pleasure and a sense of belonging, not to report marital strife, arrests for DUI, or other personal setbacks. If you can't say anything nice or at least neutral, you better not say anything. Consider how you would feel, and if you have the slightest doubt, ask.

❋ The economics of family newsletters. Putting out a family newsletter can be expensive. Not just one-time costs for a computer, printer, scanner, and all the endless and handy accessories, but recurring costs for postage, printing, phoning, and paper. You can easily spend five hundred dollars a year on a quarterly newsletter. On the other hand, a hobby like golf can easily run two or three times that, and you can't even play golf in the winter. Make a budget that fits for you, and stick fairly close to it.

If you're rich, buy all the equipment, the best of everything, and go to it. If you're not rich, however, it makes sense to start with what you've got, rent or borrow what you must, and don't buy until you're well established as a going concern. Get a good, reliable, and cheap long-distance carrier so that you can call people easily and reasonably.

Don't expect to make any money, or enough money to even defray your expenses—not the first few years. That shouldn't be your goal. This isn't to say that you shouldn't try to get some financial help from those who are benefiting from your efforts, but don't insist on it or you might kill the project. Hope that they'll begin to see the value of what you're doing. To ask people to pay twenty dollars a year for a newsletter they didn't ask for is a bit much, but if you can get your family to underwrite some or all of your expenses, so much the better. A little money never hurt anything.

Now, as to equipment. If you own a computer and are reasonably computer literate (and who can say more?), you may already know how to do desktop publishing. But for the rest of us, I need to explain myself a little.

Just a few short years ago, creating a newsletter or newspaper was complicated and expensive. But copying machines and computers have changed all that. Even renting the equipment you can now put out a newsletter for a tenth of what it used to cost. And you can do it yourself.

❋ Where do you get stories? What should you put in a newsletter? Here's a rule of thumb that works for many family newsletter editors: devote about a fourth of your space to "ancient" history—that part of your family that's dead. Devote another fourth to the oldest living members, another fourth to the generation in the saddle, and a fourth to the children. That's just a rough gauge, of course, but if you try to stay with it, you'll not make the mistake of appealing only to one generation.

Certainly one thing to put in your first issue is a list of the members of your family with their names, addresses, and phone numbers. This alone will endear you to everyone in the family. This type of beginning is called "refrigerator journalism," where the test of a good article is whether it is cut out by the reader and pasted to the refrigerator. If you can write articles that are interesting and useful, then you're in business. The most useful thing you can do for your family is enable them to keep in touch with each other, and that requires knowing names, addresses, and phone numbers.

A newsletter creates a community. Whenever any one of your readers is reading your newsletter, they are thinking of themselves as members of your family. They are experiencing their identity, and that's just what you want. That's what this history is for.

How you proceed to find good copy for your newsletter will depend on your own family. When checking addresses and phone numbers, ask about the news. Who just graduated, got married, had a baby, or won an award? Could they send a recent photo for your files? Send everyone a stamped and addressed envelope and maybe a little form for them to fill out that is basically a biography. Using a form rather than a blank page asking for a biography of themselves is a lot better. People will fill out a form who will never write a paragraph. Remember to ask about parents, ancestors, and children and grandchildren.

If you find yourself after a few months with far more copy that you can use, then you are in the same chair most editors are in: having plenty of material to select from and having to explain to angry contributors why you were unable to use *their* material.

Be sure to read the section of the book on interviewing and to apply your skills as a listener and talker. Interviewing is something we've been doing all our life, but it does take some thinking about how to do it well. It would help to get a good cassette recorder, as necessary a journalistic tool as a pad of paper and a pencil. It is also possible to get telephone/answering machines now that have a recorder built in that will tape both sides of the conversation for thirty minutes or so. This is very handy, because you are then free to ask questions, and do not have to delay the interview by writing everything down. You can listen later to the tape, and then write up your story.

Many family newsletters help publicize and are fed by an annual family reunion. Reunion time should be a busy one for the editor of the family newsletter—the period to make some contacts, pass out copies of the latest issue, encourage people to send material to you, and maybe even discreetly solicit funds.

❋ Involving others in the family. Getting others to help on the first issue may be impossible, and be prepared to go it alone for the first few issues. After that, a little wheedling is in order, but bear in mind that this was your idea, not theirs. The younger readers might be more willing to help than others, at least at first; make them "Junior Editors" and put their names on the masthead—the place where you put your own name as editor and publisher, your mailing address (including an email address if you have one), and phone number. Make older readers who help "Editors" and put their name on the masthead too. Let them share in the glory if they're willing to share in the work.

What can others do? Everything: manage the circulation list, do the printing and mailing, write stories, typeset stories, and do the editing. At the very least, you will need to organize, plan, and manage, which is a fair-sized job. The fact that your assistants live many miles away doesn't matter if you're computerized and/or have a fax.

You may get "letters to the editor" before you get articles though they may not be labeled as such. You should get permission to print any letter that refers to the newsletter and is of general interest. A quick phone call is usually all that's necessary.

It is a good idea, especially in the first issue, to put in a news request form so that readers are encouraged to send in their news. However, most people probably won't respond and you'll have to phone them. This is where it helps to have helpers who have a journalistic or literary bent and who are excited by the prospect of seeing their words in print with a byline. There are such people in every family, and one of your first jobs should be to find them.

An editor is a manager, and a manager does what's necessary to get the publication out on deadline. Few family newsletters do meet deadlines, but it does help to come out regularly. The more consistent you are, the better. You'll know you have arrived when somebody at the reunion nudges you in the ribs—someone who has never contributed a thing or acknowledged the existence of your wonderful newsletter—and growls, "Where's my newsletter? You're late!"

Probably your family also has at least one genealogist or family historian besides you. This person may have or have access to family documents, letters, scrapbooks, and the like. You can render a great service to all the family by reproducing some of these in the newsletter, many of which will almost certainly be totally new to your readers.

Milt Anderson of La Habra, California, has published a family newsletter for several years. The issue shown (Fig. 3–8) is eight pages long. Early issues did not have photographs but this issue has several, all scanned in by a machine that "sees" the original photograph and translates it into information that can be put on a computer.

This issue contains a family member's memoir from World War II, a story about an upcoming family reunion in South Dakota, excerpts from family letters the editor has received, an account by the editor about babysitting a grandchild, and a page given to births, marriages, announcements to marry, achievements, and obituaries, one of them a column-long history of the deceased's life. On the back page is a family photo taken in 1953. Milt combines history with news of the present to make a handsome and professional-looking newsletter for his extended family.

☞ SUGGESTION:

Write an "editorial" for the first issue of a newsletter you send out to your extended family in which you explain why you think the family will enjoy receiving (and helping to produce) a newsletter that you will edit and publish.

Fiction: Historical, Biographical, and Autobiographical

This is a book about writing history, not fiction. Yet as we have seen the historian uses the same narrative techniques as the fiction writer

THE FAMILETTER
A FAMILY NEWSLETTER
FOR THE PEARSON AND ANDERSON FAMILIES

Issue No. 11   MHA PUBLICATIONS   August, 1995

Several 1st cousins from the Jonas Pearson family gather: (l to r) Merna Karlson, Eldon Pearson, Arlys Stanga, me, Nadine Olson, Elaine Laufmann, Hazel Klingberg, Dennis Pearson, Alice Tiller, Darrell Pearson, Vernon Pearson and Norman Pearson.

PEARSONS PICNIC IN THE PARK!

What a great day! Pearsons all over the place! Just the way it should be when a great family gets together to meet and share memories. Lots of great food. Even the weather cooperated. A little hot and muggy maybe, but enjoyed by young and old alike.

About 100 Pearsons were able to make it. There were folks from Georgia, Idaho, Colorado, California, Minnesota, Iowa, Missouri, Michigan and Washington, and of course many from South Dakota. Nearly every branch of the family was represented. We'll try to publish a list in the next issue.

Actually not too many of the family are named Pearson, but there certainly were a lot of folks named Pearson all the same.

It was over much too soon. There were several people I never got to talk to, and that's really too bad. How can time fly so fast.

And a special thanks to all those at the picnic who donated to The FAMILETTER effort. A total of $146 was collected, not including the $28 thrown in from the Pearson Reunion treasury! This will pay mailing and reproduction costs of at least 1½ issues.

To know that so many read and enjoy is gratifying. I hope to keep it on a non-subscription basis as long as possible, and these voluntary contributions help. We currently mail about 130 copies and it is a bit costly, but it's my hobby. Hobbies can be much more expensive than this.

FIG. 3–8   *The Familetter, an excellent example of an interesting family newsletter*

and sometimes even invents material for dramatic or other purposes. In a scene from your family history, for example, you might well and legitimately invent a scene that probably or at least could have happened.

Suppose that your mother told you that one of her farm memories was going to town on Saturday mornings to sell eggs to the grocer. You know for certain that she sold eggs to the grocer. Chances are that she also gathered the eggs or helped with the gathering and cleaned and packed them for sale. For one good dramatic reason or another, you might need to invent such a scene. That's perfectly permissible. Suppose also that your mother had a sister about her own age, and that the two of them played happily and, as sometimes children will, a little zanily when Mom and Dad weren't watching. Suppose in your invented scene you went a little further and put the sister in the story too, and had them playing a game of toss-the-egg-back-and-forth, and one of the eggs dropped on the floor and broke. This is all plausible enough. But now suppose even further that you knew that your grandmother was terrified of your grandfather. You speculate: what if she had come upon the two girls just as the egg dropped and, knowing that her husband would be furious because he'd notice the missing egg, she quickly grabbed a spatula and a bowl, scraped the egg from the floor, and fried it for Dad at breakfast!

Now somewhere in there we've probably crossed over into fiction, or at least into history that we'd have to encumber with so many warning signs that we may as well say we're writing fiction and be done with it. You can say that your story is "based on facts as you know them," or that you've "drawn logical inferences from the facts that you know and have tried to be true to the tenor of the reality," or something similar. It's a matter of taste. If the reader is given fair warning, what's the harm? And the good that may come of it can be substantial: an imaginative reconstruction of the family's early life.

So if you are writing about an era that is sketchy in your own memory or took place years before you were born, then you may well decide that you'd better label what you're writing as fiction.

There can be other reasons for calling your work fiction. It may be that you want to write about something in your own or your family's life that you don't feel, for any number of reasons, you can be utterly candid about. In spite of the old saying that honesty is the best policy, you may not feel you can be completely forthcoming. You might want to draw on your imagination more than the facts will allow. Maybe you want to enhance some details of your life and suppress others in order to make an imaginative statement. That's what art is all about. Most novelists write at least somewhat autobiographically. It's perfectly legitimate. You may still be open to legal action, and no matter what sort of disclaimers you issue at the preface to your work, at the next family reunion you may be asked some pointed questions.

What follows is an excerpt from a long work that is neither family history nor fiction, but something in between. The author, Annabelle Sumera of Birmingham, Michigan, is writing about her own family, and she bases her writing on the facts as she knows them. In order to render her family's history rather than merely tell about it, she has extrapolated from these facts. With the work she included a two-page outline of the bare facts of the story, and added:

> Dialogue, descriptions, and connective pieces are from my imagination. I grew up in the same location as the story so it was not too difficult to imagine the town, the store, the school, the church, etc. . . . Two of the aunts (Maggie and Mabel) were well known by me as a child. Edgar in the story was my father.
>
> My three brothers were all more familiar with the background of my father's family than I. Since I was the youngest and a girl, I was 'protected' from the realities of the hardships of my father's early life.

A Cutting from the Vine
by Annabelle Sumera

In the farm kitchen, near the black iron cookstove where the embers of the breakfast fire still sputtered, the child sat on a high stool, her tiny hands closed in fists against her chest. She scrunched her eyes tight against the compulsion to cry out as Ma combed and braided her hair, pulling ever and ever tighter against the pink scalp.

Along with the physical pain, the child was inflicted with a steady stream of words admonishing her to accept the pains of life. It was God's will that humans must suffer for their sins. She must pray to be forgiven and to ask God's help to make her worthy of a good home and parents to care for her.

The child, Mabel, did pray in her four-year-old way. She did not know what sinning meant nor why she would be forgiven. She knew only that she wished Maggie, her oldest sister, was still at home. Sometimes Maggie had scolded her and always hurried her along, but she combed her hair gently and helped Mabel get buttoned up the back. And so Mabel's prayers were disguised as wishes. The more she thought about Maggie's being gone, the more the tears gathered behind her squeezed-shut eyes.

Finally Ma was finished. "There," she said. "Now say your prayers and then you can go outside."

Dutifully, Mabel did as she was bidden, mumbling the only prayer she knew, "Now I lay me down to sleep." When she was done she murmured a soft "Amen" and slid off the stool.

As she passed William's cradle, the baby cooed and waved curled fingers. Mabel stopped and slipped her finger into one small fist. The baby gurgled and clung and Mabel would have lingered to play with him but Ma's voice interrupted sharply, "Leave the baby alone. I've told you and told you not to touch him."

Fearing further displeasure, the child hastened outside. It was early May. The yard and orchard were carpeted in yellow dandelions. A sigh shook her small body as Mabel glanced over her shoulder, fearful of being recalled to do penance for some imagined misdemeanor. With Maggie gone, she felt alone and defenseless against the presence in the house, the woman she called Ma.

Mabel knew they had not always lived in this house. She knew Ma was not their real mother. She was their stepmother, as Maggie and the others emphasized in low-toned voices.

The older sisters often told the story of how their mother, Roseann, had died when Mabel was two months old. At that time ten-year-old Maggie had tried her best to be mother to her five younger brothers and sisters. It had not been easy despite the support of friends and neighbors. Short and stocky, given to standing with arms akimbo, she bossed the younger ones and managed somehow to get food on the table. Though clothes were clean, they were not well ironed, often with scorch marks indicating the ironer's ineptness.

During the day the baby's cradle stood near wherever Maggie worked, and it was Maggie who rose to tend her at night. Thus in the baby's quickening mind, Maggie became a caregiver.

The children's father was a veterinarian although he more humbly called himself a horse-doctor. Locally he was known at Doc George. Loose limbed and relaxed, he was ready to serve whenever a farmer needed help with an ailing animal. After Roseann died, the wives of these farmers saw that, along with whatever monetary pay he received for his services, he also went home with a loaf of freshly baked bread, a package of cookies, or some other victuals hot from the oven. The children were grateful for a kettle of savory stew. At supper they wiped their bowls clean with chunks of crusty bread. Maggie's meals tended toward boiled potatoes and scrambled eggs, which no one dared complain about for fear of Maggie's tongue. She would shrilly announce that anytime they didn't like what she cooked they could jolly well do it themselves.

So they ate what Maggie prepared, did their chores at her command, and fretted for the missing presence in their motherless home. George did his best to be both father and mother, hiding his grief in the business of the farm, his doctoring, and in caring for the children, who constantly sought his company if he were available.

Cora, eight at the time of her mother's death, and Belle, seven, often fretted at washing baby diapers, sweeping floors, and generally being responsible for four-year-old Edgar and two-year-old Gar. They preferred to be off picking berries or searching in fence posts for bluebird nests. At first Maggie had insisted they stay close to the house. Later she relented and let them leave her sight.

"You can go for a while," she said, "and take Gar with you."

"Aw, Maggie," protested Belle. "Gar's too little. His legs will get tired."

"Then carry him," answered Maggie with no hint of sympathy. "Come right back when I ring the bell and bring the cows with you. Pa and Edgar'll be home by then."

Then in the stillness of the house perhaps Maggie too would find respite. She might pull Pa's rocker near the cradle where the baby slept and for a few moments cast off her heavy burdens.

Occasionally one or another of the local women dropped in to help out. From them Maggie learned improved cooking skills. How proud she was to present her father with her first apple pie.

"Best apple pie I ever ate," George praised her. Maggie's weariness vanished with his words. "Here, Pa. You can have the rest of mine." Young Edgar held out his plate.

"And mine, too," said Cora and Belle in turn. Two-year-old Gar, seeing the others holding their plates toward their father, offered his also.

"That much pie's not good for any man," said George, "but I thank you all for the thought." From each plate he took one small bite, repeating his thanks to each.

When the meal was finished, Edgar and Gar played with

a set of small blocks while the girls tidied up the supper dishes. Belle and Cora voiced their resentment of Maggie's constant bossing.

"Oh, Maggie. Leave us be. We know how to do the dishes," protested Belle. Cora added, "You certainly told us enough times."

George listened to this exchange as he rocked the baby, pausing to trace the tiny cheek and brow as if searching for a resemblance to Roseann. His dear, beloved Roseann.

Soon Gar tired of the blocks and began to fuss from end of day weariness. He climbed on his father's knee, demanding his turn to be rocked. And so the family spent their days, struggling to hold together in spite of the void in their young lives.

In the fall, Cora and Belle went off to school in their less than perfectly ironed pinafores. Edgar was ever at his father's heels. He sat on a stool in the barn while Pa milked, he threw grain to the chickens, and rode along in the buggy whenever his father was called to do doctoring. He watched and listened and asked questions, storing up knowledge which he would later make use of. Maggie's days were filled with tending the baby and Gar.

The seasons passed and George watched his children grow more ragtag, their clothes outgrown or needing mending. The baby began to toddle about, placing a great responsibility on Maggie's childish shoulders. One day George spent an hour at Roseann's graveside and came away determined to find a solution.

On August 30, 1887, George married Ann, the sister of a local man with whom he regularly did business. Ann was a reclusive person little given to casual chit-chat, silently moving about as she did her share of the chores in her brother's household. Obedient to her brother John, she accepted the marriage arrangement though George at thirty-eight was her senior by fifteen years. It was a year and a month since Roseann had died.

After a simple ceremony and a short stay at the hotel in Arthur, Ontario, George brought Ann home and presented her to his family.

The children were watching on the veranda when their father arrived. They watched silently as he helped Ann from the buggy. She paused for a minute and readjusted her skirt as she faced the waiting children. Ann was a tall young woman. From a center part her hair was pulled severely back to a bun low at the nape. Straight brows and sallow skin intensified deep-set eyes, sometimes hazel, sometimes darker. With his hand at Ann's elbow, George began the introductions.

"Children, this is your Ma. Maggie, take your Ma's coat."

"Yes, Pa." Maggie ducked her head in greeting and reached for the black broadcloth wrap. She gave no direct greeting to the woman her father had called Ma.

And down the line George went, "This is Cora. And that is Gar hiding behind her skirts."

"Pleased to meet you," Cora said, trying to draw Gar forward. He clung more tightly, burying his face against her leg.

"And this is Edgar, my right-hand man, and this is Belle." George smiled at his brood, noting that they had prepared for this meeting with clean faces and combed hair. Then he stooped and lifted the little one. She turned shyly toward Ann, her finger in her mouth.

"This is our baby, Roseann," said George to his wife. "We call her Rosie." He stepped toward Ann as if expecting her to reach for the child, but Ann's arms remained at her sides, her lips unsmiling.

"No," she said, her voice low and unaccented. "We will neither call her Roseann nor Rosie. I have already decided. Her name will be Mabel."

A small gasp came from Maggie, her shoulders stiffened. "But she's named for our mother," she said, her face flushed, defiant. Two pairs of eyes met and held. The clash of wills was broken only when George set the child at Maggie's feet and said, "It's all right, Maggie. It's probably better this way. Take Ro—Mabel in. Belle, show your Ma the way. Cora and Edgar, come with me. We've some things to bring in."

Undirected, Gar stayed on the veranda. Should he run after his father and the others or enter the house with this new and strange person? His three-year-old curiosity won out. He followed Belle into the house.

Out in the orchard, the child, Mabel, sat in a patch of golden dandelions trying to make a chain as Maggie had taught her. Off and on she tugged at her hair, attempting to ease the pull at her scalp. Gradually the hair relaxed and she concentrated on the chain, only to give up when her small fingers proved too inept. She turned her attention to the hollow dandelion stems, splitting them from the ends with her tongue and admiring the coiled designs that resulted. She wished she could show the blossoms and curls to Maggie but Maggie was not at home.

Only yesterday Mabel had sat on the bed and watched as Maggie folded freshly washed and ironed white cotton petticoats and handkerchiefs, two pairs of black lisle stockings, and her everyday dress of blue and white checked gingham. Her Sunday clothes, a navy skirt and a white dimity blouse, would be folded and packed last.

Occasionally Maggie interrupted her packing to hug the sniffling Mabel, who pleaded with her not to go. Maggie assured her that everything would be all right.

"You're going to be just fine, sweetpea. Cora and Belle will take care of you. And Pa's always here."

Mabel was not reassured but the sniffling gave way when Maggie brought a small box from the dresser drawer. It held her special things: an ivory comb and brush set, hairpins, a sachet of rose petals still faintly fragrant, and a tortoise-shell comb.

Maggie tucked the comb in Mabel's hair. "This belonged to our real mother," she said. "I want you to love her even though you don't remember her. Let's look at her picture once more before I leave."

Going to the hall, Maggie listened at the head of the stairs. The only household sound was the intermittent whir of the sewing machine. She returned to the big room which the four girls shared. Reaching behind the dresser she drew out the portrait of a gentle-faced woman with searching dark eyes beneath straight brows. The closed lips turned up at the corners in the slightest suggestion of a smile.

"This is your real mother," she whispered. "Her name was Roseann, just like yours used to be."

The tortoise-shell comb slipped as Mabel slid from the bed. She caught it and held it clutched against her chest as she stood wide-eyed in front of the portrait. The picture was familiar to her. It was a regular routine for Maggie or one of the other girls to keep it clean and dusted. Mabel was frequently included in this ritual during which the girls extolled the loving, caring mother of their early childhood. These comments gave a deeper dimension to the black-and-white portrait. It came to have a life of its own.

Mabel knew they had not always lived in this house. She had no recollection of her own; she just assumed those told by her sisters. Many times she had heard the story of the day they moved here and Ma and Maggie had fought over the picture. Now her small body tensed as her own subconscious memory merged with the retold story.

A few months after George and Ann were married, he sensed Ann's discontent. Her moods shifted from extreme irritability to periods of withdrawal into silence. George discussed the problem with John, Ann's brother. Together the men decided a new beginning would relieve her anxiety. Through his business connections, John learned about a growing area in the thumb of Michigan. The farmland was rich and there was no veterinarian in the vicinity. And so George rented a farm midway between the small towns of Deckerville and Minden. Both were centers for the agricultural commerce around them as well as nearby lumbering activity. Each town had a railway station, drygoods stores, a hotel, and other necessaries. Deckerville was slightly larger with three churches, a high school, and an auditorium over the grocery store.

When the family arrived at the farm, they found a two-storied clapboard house, its once-white paint grayed and weathered. A wide veranda ran around two sides, shading the south and west windows from the hot afternoon sun. While they waited for the dray carrying the rest of the household goods, the children ran off to inspect the barn and other outbuildings. They stood in awe gazing up at the windmill soaring from its splayed galvanized steel legs buried deep in the ground as if rooted there.

George and Ann entered the kitchen, which opened off the veranda. Disturbed by their entering, a spider scurried across the wide plank floor. With a quick, angry motion, Ann stomped on it. "I can't stand spiders. They are so evil," she said.

"We'll get them all cleaned out in just a minute," said George. "Let's see the rest of the house."

Together they walked through the dining room, which

also opened onto the veranda, and then into the small par lor. Here the wallpaper was not so faded, its design of greei ivy climbing continuous trellises. Beyond the parlor was ; bedroom.

"This is our room," Ann said. "The children will sleep up-stairs. It's a nice house, George. Will things go well here?"

"Yes, Ann. Things will go well here." He placed a reas-suring arm about her shoulders.

Later, when the dray arrived, the children scurried about, moving what they could from wagon to house, opening boxes and crates and distributing articles through-out the rooms.

Unfortunately it was Maggie who had stripped the cov-ering from the picture of Roseann. She searched the walls of the parlor and found a nail left by the previous tenants. Pleased, she climbed on a box and hung the picture just as her stepmother entered the room.

"No!" screamed Ann. "No, no, no." She pushed Maggie from the box and dragged the picture off the wall, all the while pouring out invectives at Maggie, calling her mean and spiteful and stubborn.

"I want this picture out of my house. I want it destroyed. I'm your mother now. Do as I say!" She moved as if to smash the picture to the floor. Maggie caught hold of it and the two of them tugged for possession.

"It's mine. It's mine!" cried Maggie. She began to cry with a mixture of anger and fear.

Entering the house, George heard the racket. He viewed the scene, a stunned expression on his face, then he moved forward and placed his hand on the picture. The screaming stopped. By now the others had also gathered. They stood about in various degrees of shock. The baby began to whimper because Maggie was crying.

It had been evident to George that there was no easy as-sociation between Ann and Maggie. Their conversations were limited to the tasks at hand. Maggie resented any di-rection from Ann, and Ann was never quite satisfied with what Maggie did. If Ann said the rinse water for the white clothes needed more bluing, Maggie put in more bluing. Too much bluing. Instead of white the sheets and pillow-cases and even her father's good shirt came out faintly tinged with blue, like snow on a clear wintry evening.

Now there seemed to be open warfare.

With his hand on the picture, George asked, "What's the matter?"

Ann's eyes darkened with hidden energy. Her face distorted with rage.

"I will not have this picture in the house," she declared, her voice shrill and shaking. "I'm your wife now. This is my house."

For the first time Ann had expressed open resentment of her predecessor. George was shocked by the depth of her feeling. His first inclination was to get rid of the portrait, but then there were the children to consider. It was a picture of their mother.

George turned to Maggie. "Do as your Ma says."

"No," said Maggie, pleading. "I want this. It's our mother."

George drew a deep breath. He was caught in the middle of a conflict he had tried to ignore.

"Maggie. Take it upstairs." His voice was low and stern as he released Ann's hands from the frame. "Your Ma's tired. We'll let her rest a bit."

"She's not my Ma," countered Maggie. Nevertheless she moved toward the stairs. Belle opened the door for her and together they carried the offending article to their room. Still fearful of what might happen if it were left in open view, the girls slid it behind the dresser where it had remained ever since.

After that episode, for her father's sake, Maggie had made a conscious effort to control her temper. Whenever possible, she accepted day work away from home, leaving Cora and Belle to contend with the vagaries of the stepmother's disposition. Frequently Maggie worked for Mrs. Smither, the closest neighbor. Sometimes she took Mabel with her. Mrs. Smither made much of the little one, giving her spoons and pans to pay with while she and Maggie canned applesauce or washed clothes.

Now, at fourteen, Maggie welcomed the opportunity to escape the tension building between herself and Ma. She had pleaded with Pa to let her go with Mrs. Smither's sister in Detroit. Maggie would live with the family and take care of a new baby expected any day now.

Pa was reluctant. "It's a long way away, Maggie. It'll be for several months. You've never been away from home for that long."

"They're good people, Pa. I'll be busy and the time will go fast. Besides, I'm old enough." Maggie presented her arguments and for once Ma agreed with her.

"The girl's right, George. She's old enough to be on her own." Then to Maggie she added, "Take your Bible with you. Read it every day. Pray for strength to withstand the evils that will be all about you."

Maggie nodded to her stepmother. It was the nearest thing to a farewell the two spoke.

Maggie had interrupted her packing to comfort Mabel as they studied the portrait of their mother. Maggie talked in soothing tones in an attempt to relieve her sister's anxiety. Mabel stood before her sister, twisting a sodden handkerchief into a crumpled mass.

"You always came home at night before, Maggie. I don't want you to go. Why can't you stay here?"

"I have to go, sweetpea. It's the way I'll make some money. Then when I have a place of my own, I'll hang this in the parlor and all of you can look at it when you come to visit me." Her light, cheerful words were meant to lift the gloom from Mabel's face.

"Can I come see you, too?" asked Mabel between sniffles.

"You most of all," answered Maggie, "and then I'll always call you Roseann."

"Pa calls me 'Rosie' sometimes," whispered Mabel. Instinctively she knew this was something special that occurred only when she and her father were alone.

"I know," said Maggie, "but don't say anything to her."

Mabel gave up protesting. She leaned on the bed, forlorn and tear streaked, as Maggie replaced the picture and finished her packing. In a few minutes Pa came and tied up the carton and carried it downstairs and out to the buggy. After a quick hug, Maggie and Pa had driven off to the train station.

That was yesterday and now it was today and Mabel stood in the orchard clutching the wilting dandelions. She gazed toward the road as if she might see Pa and Maggie return as Maggie had always done before at day's end. This time she would not. There was an emptiness in Mabel's young life she did not understand. Maggie had left and now Mabel knew she did not like leavings.

☞ SUGGESTION:

Write a scene from the life of the earliest ancestor you know anything about. That might be a grandparent or even someone from an earlier period. If you don't have an idea for a scene from their life, show them getting dressed in the morning or eating a meal or anything else that they're likely to have done. Invent freely, based on your best hunch as to what they might really have been like. Then decide whether you have written history or fiction or something in between.

Printing and Publishing
Your Family History

What Do You Do with What You've Written?

Let's assume that by the time you've read this far you have written a manuscript of family history. Even if you have limited your writing to the suggestions I've made along the way you should have a thick sheaf of pages. But the thought of printing those pages, which may seem expensive and involved, may tempt you to do nothing with them, letting your manuscript gather dust until someone else comes along and does the work. "Let the heirs do that part," one old fellow said to me with a laugh.

That's not always the way things turn out. Sometimes what happens is that someone else comes along and tosses it out, so the work you've done benefits no one but yourself. That would be a shame, because you wrote this work at least in part for your family to read and enjoy.

You may have a very modest view of the work you've done and may not consider it particularly worthy of publication. Even if you may think it's an act of presumption to print your own work, make a backup copy of the manuscript and put it in a secure place like a safety deposit box or another family member's home.

During World War II my father was stationed in North Africa and Italy and wrote hundreds of letters home to his wife and two sons. The letters were a priceless family possession. We kept them in an old Army trunk in the basement and a few years ago someone stole the trunk. We never saw it or the letters again. What a sad outcome for our family! Of course we hadn't transcribed the letters or made copies of them. As a result, some of our heritage has been forever lost. It is very important to copy your manuscript and any other family documents you have and put the copies in a safe place different from the location of the originals.

Printing Your History Easily and Cheaply

Your best option is to go ahead with self-publication. This book is about writing family history and not publishing it per se, but publication is so important that I am going to discuss some of the considerations. You should also look over one or more of the books in Appendix A about printing and publishing that go into much more detail.

I would also suggest you look at what others like you have done. Ask around at your local public library, historical society library, or county genealogical society library to find some good examples.

Just a few short years ago, self-publishing a book was a rich person's game costing thousands of dollars. I know a gentleman who wrote a book in the 1950s about his life and opinions and had it self-published at a cost of four thousand dollars, a very substantial chunk of money back then, enough to buy a new Cadillac or make a down payment on a house. He distributed a few copies to friends and relatives and sold some at four dollars a copy. When I met him forty years later he was ninety-three years old and still had a few copies left in the closet of his room at the nursing home. I bought one for three dollars.

Until the last decade or so, it was rare for anyone to write a book, and rarer still for anyone to self-publish it. That's not true anymore. Technology has changed everything. I know a man who writes and publishes a book of his poems and essays every year and gives copies to friends. The copying machine and computer revolution have made it possible for many people to easily write and publish a book.

Using Photos

The first step in publication is to make your manuscript look more like a book. For the moment, don't worry about whether you've written the manuscript in longhand, typed it on a typewriter, or done the work on a computer. How to work the text over and get it into shape for publication can come later. More important now is decide how to make use of some of those family photos.

I'm surprised at how often I see family history books that lack photographs or use only a few. Including photographs complicates publication and increases your costs, but they do much to make the book more readable and useful.

Printing the family photographs can help the entire family enjoy, appreciate, and benefit from your photos. Imagine an art museum that held great pictures and took good care of them but never displayed them! That's what you have in that shoebox or desk drawer full of old family photos. What are those photos worth if no one sees them?

Laying Out Your Book

Here are some of the ways to put in as many photos as you can afford to:

1. Place your photos with the text as they are relevant. Along with the discussion of the years you lived in the house on Elm Street, for example, put the photo of the house. You can wrap the text around the photograph. *Lightly* paste the actual photograph in the place you've made for it. Use just a spot of paste on the back of the photo—just enough to hold it in place during the printing. For a sharp reproduction that often looks just as good as the original photograph, have the copy shop make a laser color copy (it doesn't matter whether the photo is black and white or color, "laser color copy" only refers to the kind of machine used; it will do a fine job of color or black and white). These are fairly expensive but affordable if you are only making a few books. You may even wish to "gang" several photographs onto one page—the copy shop will charge by the page, not by the picture—then cut out that photo and paste it in the actual book.

2. Have the copy shop scan the photo. In this process the photograph is scanned by the machine and turned into data that goes into a computer so the picture can be printed out.

3. Make your photos into halftones that are then printed by a "regular" offset printer and inserted at relevant places in the book as separate pages. Halftones will be expensive but of very high quality, and the more books you print the cheaper their cost will be.

4. Make photographs of your photos and then paste them into the book. This is an obvious but often overlooked option when you are making only a half-dozen books or so.

However you use photographs, be sure to put captions with them if they are not explained in the text immediately adjacent. Do not insert photos without captions or readers will have no idea of their significance.

Don't overlook other kinds of graphics for your book, either. Your book will also be enhanced by your own work, even if it isn't "professional" quality. Remember, the standard here is authenticity. Would you rather have a book by your mother that is decorated with her drawings and designs, or one by some nameless and slick artist who was hired to do the job?

Items that you may have in your possession or have access to may copy or photograph well and should be included. Diplomas, naturalization papers, grants of land, and so on may be pertinent and interesting. You may wish to photograph some family heirlooms such as furniture or jewelry.

How you put text, headings, photos, and other graphics together in your book is the layout. Whatever you take to the copy shop for printing, they will follow; lay the whole book out the way you want it to look.

Don't crowd the pages. It's better to have too much white space than too little.

If you wonder what a page or your cover is going to look like, run one copy and take a look. Pin it up on the wall and live with it for a few days, just as you might do with a wallpaper sample. Take your time.

Use one or two typefaces, but not more. If you want additional variety, consider using italic styles of the same typeface. Too many different typefaces can appear amateurish and confusing.

Proofread several times carefully, and have others proofread too. The printer will not proofread for you. It can be extremely upsetting to shell out a lot of money for a beautiful book and have a typographical error on the cover. There will be some errors in the text no matter how much you proofread and proofread that you will have to live with, but check and double-check the high profile areas like the cover, table of contents, and captions under photographs. Some common errors are transposing words, having the wrong caption under a photo, misidentifying a person in a caption, misspelling names, and using wrong dates. In one of my issues of *LifeStory*, I added twenty-seven years to the age of a writer simply by transposing 1930 into 1903. He was very understanding, but not everybody is.

The Types of Publication

❋ The "vanity" publisher.   The one kind of publisher or printer I would urge you to avoid is the "vanity" or subsidy publishing house, so-called because they appeal to your desire to be a published author. The vanity publisher advertises that it will print, bind, publish, advertise, and distribute your book just as any commercial publishing house would—for a price. And that's the catch; the publisher risks nothing. A nonsubsidized publisher risks a lot, and that's why it is so hard to get one to publish a manuscript. The vanity publisher asks *you* to take the risk.

Be careful about vanity presses. Read what others have to say, talk to a lawyer before you enter into any contract, and pay special attention to what the company promises to do about marketing your book. The fine print may allow it to put the tiniest of ads in the most obscure of publications and call that marketing.

❋ The publisher for hire.   There is another kind of publication in which you pay for the printing that is quite another story. These companies agree to print, bind and "publish" by delivering a certain number of copies directly to you. You may also ask the company to take your copy and put it into an attractive format. Many commercial printers will do this, as well as small publishing houses who may contract out the printing or do it themselves.

Some of these companies will even help with the editing or writing, or even write it for you. Generally, I encourage you to write your own book if you possibly can. In cases where this is impossible—for health reasons, for example—a good ghostwriter can be useful. A good, businesslike, and professional ghostwriter will be up-front with you about charges. Expect to pay a ghostwriter pretty well; it's a complex and rare skill to be able to write someone else's life story.

❋ The commercial publisher.   A third kind of commercial publication is the kind we all think of when we think of an author getting a work published: the nonsubsidized commercial publisher who pays you money in the form of royalties and (possibly) an advance or grant. The royalty will probably be a small percentage of the price of the book, but the publisher pays you—not the other way around. Should you try for this kind of publication?

The tone in the commercially oriented publication is likely to be less intimate. If you write your book with the world-as-audience in mind (particularly the book-buying world), you may adversely affect your work as a family history—like the difference between speaking in public at a luncheon and speaking around the kitchen table at dinner with your family. A book that's valuable commercially *may* be less valued in the family.

On the other hand, let's say that you feel at the end of your book that you've got a saleable product. Why not try for as wide an audience as possible and make some money? Why not try for a little fame?

Start by getting a copy of the current annual issue of *Writer's Market*. Probably your library's reference shelf will have it. Turn to the section on book publishers and start reading. Step one is to find the right publisher to send your manuscript to. Step two might be to ask any friends who have published or have tried to publish a book their opinion. Talk to the book editor of your local paper, teachers and others who may have had dealings with publishing houses. Take a look at some of the literature on the subject (see bibliography).

Expect to do a lot of waiting. It may take months for your manuscript to be evaluated and possibly rejected; it will take many more months for it to get into print. Even if published, don't be astonished if you don't make a huge splash.

❋ You as commercial publisher. If you are getting the impression that I think commercial publication can be a waste of time, you're right. An alternative route would be to publish the book yourself by the means described below. Then, if you're still feeling commercial, give a few copies to book reviewers of local and regional papers. Send them a review copy along with a personal letter. Follow up in a week or ten days with a phone call. Most larger papers will only rarely review a self-published work, but smaller hometown papers may figure it's news that you published a book. Try to get local bookstores to carry it. Offer to put a few copies there on consignment. Be businesslike, friendly, and modest. Who knows? Maybe your book will take off.

Obviously, if your book is about your life as a lion-tamer or your years as an explorer in the Yukon, you have a lot better chance of selling your book than you do if it's your observations about life or your political opinions (a surefire dustcatcher) or your recommendations for improving the community's building code. If you have an unusual and interesting point of view, you may be launched on a great new career.

Publishing yourself will not hurt your chances to publish commercially, and may even help them. Jessie Foveaux, whom I mentioned earlier in this book, one of my first adult writing students in the 1970s, wrote the story of her life and her family's life and printed just enough copies for her children and grandchildren. They read it avidly and talked about it with friends and neighbors. Naturally the friends wanted to read the book too.

Though the book is addressed to her family, over the years she has received orders through the mail from several hundred strangers wanting to buy a copy. Reluctantly, she has supplied them with copies, though she insisted on selling the book for very close to what it costs her to produce it.

Self-Published Family History Books

Books as physical objects vary in size, the number of pages, the mix of text and graphics, and binding. There seem to be as many varieties of publication as there are family histories. Many family history books are in a 8½-by-11-inch trim size. This is a very common size because no cutting or folding is involved. Most copy shops can produce a book like that within a few hours or a day. About twenty rectangular holes are punched by a machine in the left side and a plastic binding is installed.

The example shown in Fig. 4–1 is 8½-by-11 inches with eighteen pages printed on one side only. About half of them are text and were printed in a copy shop; the rest are all photographs with brief captions. The photos are of high quality and were printed by an offset printer. The cover is what is called "cardstock," which is a heavy paper. The book is the story of the author's parents' youth, their meeting, their settling on a farm in Kansas, the rearing of their children there, and the last years of their lives. The last paragraph of the text of the book concludes simply,

> On February 2nd, 1947, when Charlie died, they [Charlie and Ida, the author's parents] had been married almost sixty years. Rather than continue to live out on the farm and in a big house, Ida moved into Burrton, next door to daughter Lillian and Earl Frederick. After the death of Lillian, Ida purchased a small new house in Burrton and lived there the remainder of her life. Both Ida and Charlie outlived all their brothers and sisters. They had good health most of their lives and they both were active people with a keen interest in national and world affairs. The children, and their descendants, have received from them a great heritage.

Ida, Charlie, Lillian, Irene
and Raeburn
around   1900

FIG. 4—1   *Inez Howard's biography/history of her parents' lives together on the
family farm in Kansas. Several family photographs were reproduced by an
offset printer using halftones.*

I have also seen a number of very attractive books that are basically three steel-ring binders with pages typed and inserted and with photographs pasted in. Lula Leverenz of Windom, Minnesota, made a book like this for each of her six children. It was obviously a labor of love.

You can buy different kinds of bindings. Bob Joyce of Hawthorne House, a publishing and ghostwriting firm in Santa Ana, California, used a simple compression binding with two aluminum bolts through the pages to hold the front and back of the book together. I have a copy of *They Called Me Kitty*, a book he made for his mother. Discount stores, book and stationery stores, and many photographic supply stores sell these as photo albums. Joyce removed the plastic photo pages and inserted printed pages along with some pages of photos that were laser color copied. Anyone with access to a computer and a copy shop could make such a book.

FIG. 4–2   *Bob Joyce of Hawthorne House produced his mother's autobiography,* They Called Me Kitty. *Its binding is a ready-made photo album available in photo supply departments. The book was written and laid out on a computer.*

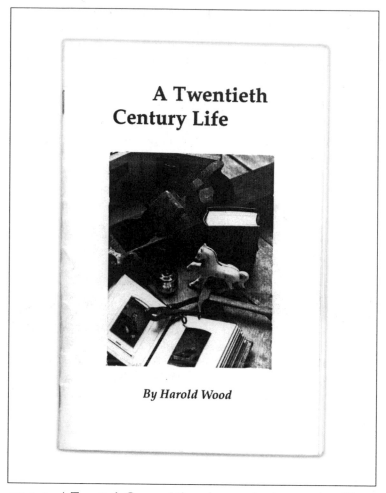

FIG. 4–3   A Twentieth Century Life *employs a cardstock cover and a saddle-stitched binding.*

The binding of this little book is "saddle-stitched," which is a printer's way of saying it's stapled together. It has only a few photographs, but the author's meticulous account of his farming years in Wisconsin is engrossing. The book has twenty-six pages and a cardstock cover (see Fig. 4–3). The author, who was about eighty when he wrote the book, had some additional thoughts and recollections later on and so he wrote a second book.

Good Luck!

If you have made it this far, we have come a long way together. I hope this book helps you write for your family. Please give a copy of your book to your local historical society and library. You may not consider your life of any historical importance beyond your family, but professional historians who use these facilities may feel differently.

Consider including a comment page in your book for your relatives and friends to fill out and send to you. Put a dotted line to indicate where they can use a razor knife to cut it out. These comments might become the basis for another book. You may spark a "round robin" of books or a future edition. You might want to print an addendum or even start a family newsletter. Your book will certainly stimulate an interest in family history among the members of your family.

Be prepared to have family members freely criticize what you've done. Fortunately, most people are pleasantly surprised at the reaction they get from family members. One man I know handed out copies of his family history at a reunion and to his surprise everyone sat down and started reading it right then and there—"It almost spoiled the reunion," he said. "Everyone just sat around reading." He hadn't expected them to read it ever, much less on the spot. But like any other human enterprise, writing and publishing a book is fraught with risk as well as reward. May your risks be surmounted easily and your rewards be large and long lasting.

Resources for the Family Historian

This list of titles reflects my own experience. Many of the books about family history in the average public library are outdated. They may still be worth reading, but anything written before about 1980 will not reflect the computer and copier revolution that has influenced not only the way we publish family history but also how we write it. By including this list I hope I'm not implying that you must read or look at anything here in order to get on with your life story. A little research in the field is fine and probably necessary for the teacher, but there's no learning experience to match sitting down and writing.

On the other hand, if you're going to avoid writing (as we all do at times), reading or looking over these materials is probably a better way to avoid it than watching TV. I am haunted by a scene from a novel in which a man is doing research preparatory to writing a book. He has been doing the research for many years and he has filled an entire room with file cabinets containing index cards and other information. But he hasn't yet started the book.

This scene would be funny except that I have met people who have done nearly as much. I'm a little that way myself. It's hard sometimes to know where to draw the line and get on with the writing. When do we stop thinking and finding out what others think, and when do we start writing and saying what we think? You're the only one who can answer that question for yourself.

BIRREN, JAMES E., and DONNA E. DEUTCHMAN. 1991. *Guiding Autobiography Groups for Older Adults: Exploring the Fabric of Life.* Baltimore: Johns Hopkins University Press.
Teachers and anyone researching the uses of autobiography may find this

book helpful. Like much scholarly social science, the prose is unnecessarily abstract, but the ideas are good.

DANIEL, LOIS. 1991. *How to Write Your Own Life Story: A Step-by-Step Guide for the Nonprofessional Writer*. 3rd ed. Chicago: Chicago Review Press.

This text has some good examples of the writings of ordinary people. I particularly liked her chapter called "Your Stories Don't Have to Be 'Stories.'"

EVANS, FANNY-MAUDE. 1984. *Changing Memories into Memoirs*. New York: Barnes and Noble.

There is lots to disagree with here, but some of her tips and technical comments about writing make the book worthwhile.

FARBER, BARRY. 1987. *Making People Talk*. New York: William Morrow.

A great book on interviewing.

FLETCHER, WILLIAM. 1989. *Recording Your Family History: A Guide to Preserving Oral History Using Audio and Video Tape*. Berkeley, CA: Ten Speed Press.

There are many suggestions for what to ask about and good information on interviewing generally.

FULWILER, TOBY, ed. 1987. *The Journal Book*. Portsmouth, NH: Heinemann.

If you've discovered or want to discover the many delights and dimensions of journaling, you'll want to read this collection of essays by teachers and writers about their experiences using journals.

GOULDRUP, LAWRENCE P. 1987. *Writing the Family Narrative*. Salt Lake City, UT: Ancestry.

This book is especially for those who are ready to write about their family's distant past.

GREENE, BOB, and D. G. FULFORD. 1993. New York: Doubleday. *To Our Children's Children*.

This book contains many stimulating suggestions for what to write about but not much else.

JOYCE, ROBERT D. 1994. *Memory Bank Notebook*. Santa Ana, CA: Hawthorne House (1509 S. Raitt St., #C, Santa Ana 92704).

This is a fill-in-the-blank workbook for the family historian and an excellent way to get started writing.

LEDOUX, DENIS. 1993. *Turning Memories into Memoirs*. Lisbon Falls, ME: Soleil Press.

There is a lot on writing as therapy and the book may be too literary for some tastes, but it has good, intelligent advice.

LOMASK, MILTON. 1986. *The Biographer's Craft*. New York: Harper and Row.

Written for those who want to learn how to write biographies of public persons rather than for family historians, it is still a useful discussion of how to tell the story of a life and therefore worth a look.

METZGER, DEENA. 1992. *Writing for Your Life: A Guide and Companion to the Inner Worlds.* San Francisco: Harper.
If you get involved in writing as a way of exploring yourself, take a look at this book.

PETERSON, MARY LOU. 1992. *Gift of Heritage.* Minneapolis: Mary Lou Productions (POB 17233, Minneapolis, MN 55417).
An interesting and sensible videotape about how to do a family history video.

POLKING, KIRK. 1995. *Writing Family Histories and Memoirs.* Cincinnati, OH: Better Way Books.
A potpourri of useful information from researching to writing to publishing; it is slanted somewhat toward the aspiring professional writer.

ROSENBLUTH, VERA. 1990. *Keeping Family Stories Alive: A Creative Guide to Taping Your Family Life and Love.* Point Roberts, WA: Hartley and Marks.
A good introduction to audio- and videotaping members of your family.

STILLMAN, PETER R. 1989. *Families Writing.* Cincinnati, OH: Writer's Digest Books.
For the growing family that values writing—journals, letters, stories, and poetry.

THOMAS, FRANK P. 1984. *How to Write the Story of Your Life.* Cincinnati, OH: Writer's Digest Books.
Covers most of the questions that occur to the beginning life writer and contains lots of ideas for topics.

Seniors' magazines and newspapers nearly always publish some family histories or autobiographical "remember when" writing, as do some local general-news newspapers. I know of at least four national periodicals that regularly publish family history of the kind described in this book:

Good Old Days is a monthly nostalgia magazine that has been around for years. It is published by House of White Birches, 306 East Parr Road, Berne, IN 46711.

Grit is another old-timer and seems to be especially rural in its orientation. It is published by Stauffer Magazine Group, 1503 SW Forty-Second Street, Topeka, KS 66609.

LifeStory is my own monthly interactive newsletter/magazine that I bill as "the family history writers' workshop." It is published by The LifeStory Institute, 3591 Letter Rock Road, Manhattan, KS 66502.

Reminisce is a bimonthly color magazine with beautiful photographs that evoke memories of the good old days. It is published by Reiman Publications, P.O. Box 998, Greendale, WI 53129.

Starting a Family History Writing Group

Writing is a lonely job. Writers, even experienced writers, benefit from reading their work to others and getting feedback. But it's not a good thing to have feedback with every line you write. In one of Albert Camus's novels, there is a character who works all day on one line and then rushes around all evening asking friends what they think of it. Naturally he goes back to work the next morning on the same line. This is no way to write a book. There is a time when feedback is out of place and unhelpful. Most writers like to get their project going and get the concept evolved before they run anything by a reader. Most of us benefit from knowing now and then what others think of what we are doing—whether we are on the right track, whether we're being informative and entertaining, or whether we're simply off on the wrong path.

Starting a family history writers' group is easy. You do not need a professional to lead you. A group can go on for years and years. Though a group can start with only two persons, more would be better. The main problem with very small groups is that if a few members can't come, then the group may be unable to function. If there are too many people, of course, the critiquing can become impersonal and intimidating.

Let's say you start with a group of three or four. Allow about two hours for your meeting. You may wish to meet in one another's homes, especially at first. You will probably be wise to pass the leadership each time, though leaving too much to the leader doesn't work well either. No group does well if everybody expects somebody else to do the work of organizing, initiating, arranging, phoning, and providing refreshments.

After your group is launched and grows in size, you may want to meet in a public room. Most communities have one or more places where noncommercial groups may meet for little or no charge. A library meeting room, a senior center, a church basement, or a community house all work well. A quiet room with a blackboard and desks or chairs with writing arms is great.

You may feel that without a teacher you are unaware of what good family history is. Read publications that regularly publish family history like *Grit, Good Old Days, Reminisce,* or *LifeStory.* And trust your own instinct: if you enjoy someone else's story, try to say what things are good and then emulate those in your own writing.

Let's say you have your first meeting simply by inviting a couple of friends you know to be interested in family history over to your house for a meeting. Ask them to bring a favorite family photograph and a pen and paper. Start the meeting by asking each person to talk about their experiences with writing (or taping) family history. Is there a family history for your family now in existence? A genealogy? Have you written or taped some stories? Let the talk flow. Then ask everyone to be quiet and do some writing based on the photograph each person brought. Ask them to write a least a page or two as a caption (see the chapter on captioning). Allow twenty or thirty minutes to do the writing. This is a good time to have coffee and cookies out.

When everyone has finished writing, give them a few minutes to loosen up by talking among themselves about how the writing went. Then ask one person to read her or his writing out loud, passing around the photo at the same time. Volunteer to go first if the others are shy about it.

Read carefully in a conversational tone. Since you have only one copy, it may be necessary to read the caption twice. When you have finished reading, ask everyone to comment. Do not ask for criticism or a critique. Ask for comments. Some will probably be critical in the worst sense and point out "mistakes" or what they think the writer did "wrong."

It's worth remembering that criticism actually means to "find the value of." Try to get everyone to make a comment. Draw them out without being pushy or intimidating. Some will undoubtedly say bland things like "I liked it." Try to get them to say why they liked it—what part did they like best? The most important goal is to find what works and point it out to the writer. Read the appendix on teaching family history writing for pointers on evaluating someone's writing. Even if you don't intend to be the teacher, in a group like this you are the teacher when you're talking. Keep in mind what you think is good family history and be willing to discuss this with the others. There's no need to achieve unanimity in this definition—it's just a way to know what others think is good.

Writing together is a healthy thing, but don't limit yourself to that. Bring material you wrote at home and read it too. You may even want to provide others with copies so that they can come to the meeting prepared to comment. This saves some time and may be necessary as your group gets larger. But it's important, too, to at least sometimes have individuals read their own work aloud as a significant learning experience and to add to the variety and personality of the meeting.

At the very least, a group like this gets you writing. You also develop your ideas and values about writing family history, gain encouragement to write at other times, and might possibly form some enduring relationships with others. Thelma Kramar, a teacher of family history writing in California, says she tries "to bond people together in appreciating each other's lives." To "appreciate each other's lives" is in itself a pretty good reason for writing family history.

Teaching Others to Write Family History

Many of the teachers of family history writing in community education programs, retirement communities, care homes, and elsewhere are professional teachers. Teaching family history writing isn't greatly different from any other subject except that usually the learners are adults who are taking the course for pleasure.

Those who have little or no formal teaching experience and are called upon to lead a group in writing family history may feel intimidated. I suggest that you think of yourself as a coach. A coach tries to get the best out of a player and tries to show that player how to do even better what he or she already does well or has the capacity to do well. A coach deals not so much with what every player should be like but with what each particular player can do. Naturally a coach would like every player on a basketball team to be able to shoot well from forty feet out, handle the ball brilliantly, be a great team player, be a scrappy defense person, and show charisma in post-game interviews. But the fact is that one player may be a great shooter yet only a moderately good or even poor team player. This doesn't mean the coach should ignore the player's need to improve but rather that the coach should focus on shooting rather than trying to make the player into something unattainable.

For example, in teaching memoir writing one often finds a writer who has an excellent eye for detail and for accurate reporting of history but who rambles. You could show the student how passages ramble and point out that the student shouldn't do that. Chances are then the student will take affront—will not hear the good comments and will withdraw by not really being there except in body or literally withdraw by not coming back.

It works better to point out to the student the wealth of detail shown on a given topic and ask for more of that detail on the same subject. Of course, this is an indirect way of saying to not ramble. You also have to mean really that you do want more detail or the student will sense your insincerity, feel patronized, and subsequently withdraw and not learn further.

Being a teacher is a subtle business, and I've taught plenty of classes where I felt the students who fell asleep got the most out of the class. On the other hand, some students may meet you years later who say your class made all the difference. That's when you feel your cup runneth over.

If you'd like to comment on *For All Time* I hope you'll take the trouble to write to me personally at The LifeStory Institute, 3591 Letter Rock Rd., Manhattan, KS 66502-9317. I'll answer every letter. Thank you!